There are clean riddles:

When is a door not a door?
When it is a jar (ajar).

There are raunchy riddles:

What was Moby Dick's father's name?
Papa Boner!

Which did you laugh at harder?

I rest my case . . .

I hope you will enjoy this collection as much as I enjoyed putting it together. Each section concludes with a multiple-choice quiz, to test your "riddlebility" as you progress through this Master Level Coarse. I call it a Master Level Coarse because jokesmithing is something I have mastered, on occasion my head is level, and trust me,* it is coarse.

Have fun, and I'll see you with my next *Pinnacle* publication.

Thanks!

Jackie "922-WINE" Martling

*Yiddish equivalent of a very prevalent American colloquialism

Other Pinnacle Books by Jackie Martling

JUST ANOTHER DIRTY JOKE BOOK

Raunchy Riddles

JACKIE MARTLING

PINNACLE BOOKS **NEW YORK**

This is a work of fiction. All the events portrayed in this book are fictional, and any resemblance to real people or incidents is purely coincidental.

RAUNCHY RIDDLES

Copyright © 1984 by Jackie Martling

An original Pinnacle Books edition, published for the first time anywhere.

First printing/July 1984

ISBN: 0-523-42275-X

Can. ISBN: 0-523-43270-4

Printed in the United States of America

PINNACLE BOOKS, INC.
1430 Broadway
New York, New York 10018

9   8   7   6   5   4   3   2   1

RAUNCHY RIDDLES

I.

What would you call a guy with no arms and no legs who can play five different instruments??
"Stump the Band"!!!

Why did the newlywed husband kiss his wife goodbye on the snatch before he went to work each day?
Because her breath was so bad in the morning!

★

Why are anchovies like telephones?
They're the next best thing to being there!

★

Why doesn't Nancy Reagan take *One-A-Day Multiple Vitamins*?
She can't figure out the dosage!

★

What does a country girl do for birth control?
If she can, she crosses her legs . . .
If she can't, she crosses her fingers!

★

Why aren't Jewish American Princesses jealous that Jewish men get circumcised and they don't?
It's no skin off their noses!

★

What's sadder than a honeymoon bride crying because it hurts?
A honeymoon bride crying because it *doesn't* hurt!

★

Why was the Chinese streetwalker starving?
No one had a yen for her!

3

Why do Black mailmen always get back to the post office so late?
Because their roots are so long!

★

How did the Polish ballplayer get ruptured?
He caught a line drive on the fly!

★

Why were the two ants running along the box top?
Because it said "TEAR ACROSS DOTTED LINE!"

★

Why was the Duchess on her knees?
She was down for the Count!

★

Why did the New Yorker cross the road? ·
Go fuck yourself!

★

What would you call a first-person investigative report on golden showers?
I Am Curious, Yellow!

★

What should a girl do if she's looking for a passionate husband?
Try a few on for sighs!

★

What's black and crisp and hangs from the ceiling?
A do-it-yourself electrician!

Why do Jewish American Princesses get married?
Because their vibrators won't take them shopping!

What's the nicest four-letter word?
"Oooh!"

How do you revive a rodent that fell in the lake?
With mouse to mouse resuscitation!

How can you tell if an obstetrician is Greek?
When a baby is born he shoves his fist up his own ass!

What is the first major milestone in a new relationship?
The first time you eat out!

What's the next major milestone?
The first time she has you for dinner!

When do you know the relationship has leveled off?
When you start thinking about food!

How can you tell if an aging movie queen has had too many face-lifts?
Her dimples have nipples!

5

Why didn't the faggot know who got him pregnant?
He didn't have eyes in the back of his head!

What's brown and sounds like a bell?
Dung!

What would you call a Puerto Rican with herpes?
Manny Sores!

What's twenty-four women in a box?
A case of Schlitz!

How can you tell if a crab is an insomniac?
It can only sleep in snatches!

Why aren't there any gay obstetricians?
Because their boyfriends would get jealous when they spanked the babies!

What did the husband say when his bored wife announced that she was going out to "paint the town?"
"Go ahead! You've certainly got the brush for it!"

What's a pool shark?
A great way to keep your neighbors from popping over for a swim!

Why did the Polish girl get a circular bed?
So she could sleep around!

When should you stop fucking your girlfriend doggie-style?
When you catch her chasing cars!

How can you tell the novice at a nudist colony?
He sticks out like a sore thumb!

What's the French method of self-defense?
Tung Fu!

What would you call Black Siamese twins who work as gigolos?
Johnson and Johnson!

★

What would you call a parrot that eats beans?
A thunderbird!

★

Why did the girl spend her afternoons with a mobster?
Racket ball!

★

How can you tell if a rabbi is sentimental?
He keeps a scrapbook of his clippings!

7

When do you know a girl's jeans are really tight?
She's carrying her handkerchief in her mouth!

Why was the leopard frustrated?
He couldn't find the right spot!

What's green and flies over Greenwich Village?
Peter Pansy!

What's a "vagrancy brassiere?"
No visible means of support!

What's a "vagrancy brassiere?"
No visible means of support!

Where do prostitutes get their tickets?
The box officer! (Tricketron?)

What do Dr. Renee Richards and winter have in common?
Snow balls! (S'no balls! Get it?)

What did the psychiatrist say to the ugly girl?
"Keep off the couch!"

When is a man his own worst enemy?
When he commits suicide in self-defense!

8

What should you do when you're not feeling yourself?
Make sure you're feeling someone else!

How do you know gynecologists are funny?
They make the ladies crack up!

Why did the Polack sit in the bathtub with his back to the faucet?
He didn't have a plug!

What did the drunk say when he woke up in the cemetery?
"If I'm alive, how come there's a tombstone? And if I'm dead, how come I have to take a leak?"

What's worse than a centipede with athlete's foot?
Captain Hook with jock itch!

What would you call a guy who sells mobile homes?
A wheel-estate broker!

How can you tell Michael Jackson is bisexual?
He only has one leg waxed!

What did the doctor do when one of his female patients complained of never having an orgasm?
He licked that problem for her!

9

What do the gays sing in the mountains of Kentucky?
On Top of Old Stogie!

★

Why is parking in a Volkswagen so frustrating?
The back seat is so small you have to take turns!

★

What's better than making a steeple with your fingers?
Making a teepee with your peepee!

★

What does an Arab call it when he catches syphilis at the oasis?
A French Foreign Lesion!

★

What's the difference between a fat old maid and a horny old maid?
A fat old maid is trying to diet!

★

How do you know when a dog is flat?
Another dog is pumping it up!

★

Why was the Jewish golfer frustrated?
He had a lot of trouble with his short putts!

★

What is "Zen hitchhiking?"
You take a ride either way!

10

What was best about the days of the miniskirters?
When they tied their shoes, you could see their squirters!

★

What happens if people tease you too much about masturbating?
You grow callous!

★

What did one leg say to the other leg?
"Look! Shorty's trying to grow a beard!"

★

How can you tell if a pimp is Jewish?
He's up to his alligator in ass!

★

Why did the coal miner's wife start to cry when he took off his pants?
Because his pecker was clean!

★

What happens if a car in the parking lot of an Italian restaurant backfires?
Half the room surrenders!

★

What's the difference between an old cat and a kitten?
An old cat can scratch and claw, but a little pussy never hurt anyone!

★

How could you tell the Negro was a masochistic homosexual?
He was Black and blue!

11

What has twenty legs, ten cherries and flies?
Ten stewardesses drinking Tom Collins's!

What would you call an Italian slum?
A spaghetto!

Why was the prostitute with two boxes an outcast?
Because she walked around with a "holier than thou" attitude!

What's a four-letter word for "woman" that ends in "u-n-t?"
Aunt!

How do they cook on Fire Island?
With pots and pansies!

How do you keep a Polish girl from biting her nails?
Make her wear shoes!

The Papa mole, the Mama mole and the baby mole were going up the mole hole when Papa mole stopped short. What were Mama mole and baby mole doing?
Smelling molasses!

How do you get a Jewish American Princess hot?
Paste sale ads on the ceiling!

12

What do you get when you sit on a pizza?
A pizza ass!

Why is the Statue of Liberty surrounded by water?
She raised her hand and the teacher said, "No!"

What do you get when you cross an Indian with a Black?
A Sioux named "boy!"

Why don't men mind women claiming to be the foundation
of our country?
Because they know who laid the foundation!

Why shouldn't you take any shit from a Polack?
Because it might be his lunch!

The answer is "Gumbo." What is the question?
What will John Derek have to do after his teeth fall out?

What's the best thing about fucking a cowgirl?
You only have to stay on eight seconds!

What did one testicle say to the other testicle?
"Why should we hang? Dick did all the shooting!"

13

Why couldn't Leo come to the phone?
He was on another lion!

What's the cheapest method of birth control?
Put a pebble in your shoe. It'll make you limp!

What would you call a German tampon?
A twatstika!

A bald brunette went to a masquerade party wearing nothing but black gloves and black boots. What was she supposed to be?
The five of spades!

How does a sailor test the water?
He puts his finger in a Wave!

What's a Norwegian head shrinker?
A psjchiatrist!

What did the bra say to the hat?
"You go on ahead. I'm gonna give these two a lift!"

Why was the Polack afraid that his bowels were gonna get lost?
He heard that they moved almost every day!

14

What's more embarrassing than getting caught parking?
Getting caught parking alone!

★

When do people decide to become humanitarians?
When they find out that vegetarians are people who eat vegetables!

★

What would you call a male stripper who wears sequins and bells?
The Star Spangled Banana!

★

How does a Jewish American Princess charge her vibrator's batteries?
To her husband!

★

If sex is the "music of the soul," what's an orgasm?
The "gland finale!"

★

If a girl tells you that her boyfriend has the biggest pecker in the county, what can you be sure of?
She's usually full of baloney!

★

What's the greatest thing about masturbation?
It's sex with someone you love!

★

What do you get when you cross an elephant with a rhino?
Elephino!

15

What did they call the gay sheriff?
The Fastest Gums in the West!

Why didn't the Polish woman want her husband shooting craps?
She didn't know how to cook 'em!

What do you call it when they blow a fuse in Madison Square Garden during a fight?
Boxer shorts!

What's the difference between an epileptic corn husker and a hooker with diarrhea?
An epileptic corn husker shucks between fits!

Why do crabs make a handy snack?
Because you can eat them right out of the box!

What does a cautious gynecologist do?
Tries not to stirrup any trouble!

What kind of coffee does a well-endowed man drink?
Jock Full o'Nuts!

Why don't chickens wear underwear?
Because it would look fucking stupid!

Who are the three most famous Chinese virgins?
"Tu Yung Tu," "Tu Dum Tu" and "No Yen Tu!"

What do you call eight girls mooning?
Octopus!

Why wouldn't the Polish girl marry the bisexual?
She said that twice a year wasn't enough for her!

What's Helen Keller's favorite color?
Corduroy!

Why did the lady walk past the tampon dispenser?
Because she'd been through her change!

Why doesn't Ronald Reagan drink Kool-Aid?
He can't figure out how to get two quarts of water in the little envelope!

What do you call it when a girl wears a jock strap?
A make-believe ballroom!

What does a post office clerk do when he's horny?
Comes in the mail!

17

What do you do if a Kotex catches fire?
Throw it on the ground and tampon it!

Why should you guard your rear when you're in a hospital?
You're in enema territory!

Who wheezes and runs a newspaper?
Ed Asthma!

How can you tell if a bird watcher is perverted?
He's the one going off on a lark!

Why was the gigolo evicted?
His rent was due and he couldn't raise it!

What do you get when you cross a diver with a Wall Street executive?
A guy who does a full twisting double somersault off the top of the Empire State Building!

What happens if a young couple mixes up the Vaseline and the putty?
All their windows fall out!

What do you get when you cross an exhibitionist with a cop?
A guy who opens up his raincoat and beats you with his night stick!

Why was 6 mad at 7?
Because 7-8-9!

What do you get when you cross a hooker with an elephant?
A two-ton pick-up with peanuts on her breath who will never forget you!

Where do all the Chinese voyeurs come from?
Peking!

What should you do if a naked girl is banging on your door?
Let her out!

When did Tom Selleck realize that he had been sleep-walking?
When he woke up in his own bed!

How did the Jewish hooker get her fur coat?
Hole sale!

Why don't Blacks let their kids hang around with Mexican kids?
They're afraid that they'll grow up knowing how to pick their own watermelons!

Why did they have trouble collecting insurance money on a brewery worker who accidentally fell into a vat of beer and drowned?
Because witnesses said that he got out three times to piss!

★

What is a cloak?
The mating call of a Chinese frog!

★

What do you see when you look at a Soviet ballerina through a keyhole?
Russian dressing!

★

What do you find in a clean nose?
Fingerprints!

★

What happened when Aunt Kitty caught her titty in the wringer of her washer?
She invented the booby trap!

★

What's green, sits on a lily pad, and turns tricks?
A prostitoad!

★

What's the easiest way to get a date with a "ten?"
Ask out two "three's" and a "four!"

★

Why are camels called "Ships of the Desert?"
Because they're always filled with Iranian semen!

Why did the basketball player marry the midget?
He was nuts over her! (Because she loved to go up on him!)

What's black and shuffles?
A panther wearing handcuffs!

What's the best way to acknowledge a girl's birthday?
Forget her past and remember her present!

How do you know when it's really cold?
The exhibitionists are walking around describing themselves!

What's a bachelorette party?
A bachelor party where all the bachelors get et!

Why did the scoutmaster have his hand in his pocket?
He was taking a head count!

What did the girl do when her vibrator got caught inside her?
Found a friend who would reach up and change the batteries!

What does Oral Roberts do on his day off?
Teaches his dog to heal!

21

Why do mice have such small balls?
So few of them know how to dance!

★

Why did the Polack pick his nose apart?
To see how it ran!

★

What does a gynecologist say when he's tired?
"I'm bushed!"

★

If at first you don't succeed, why should you try again?
Because she expects you to!

★

How would you describe a Catholic weekend?
Payday, playday, prayday!

★

What's the definition of a "ten?"
A girl who has a flat head to rest your beer on and can suck a
golf ball through a garden hose!

★

Why did it take so long to recruit a Black astronaut?
No power windows!

★

What is Jell-O?
Kool-Aid with a hard-on!

Why should you never pee through a screen door?
Because you'll strain yourself!

★

How many mystery writers does it take to change a light bulb?
Two. One to screw it almost all the way in, and one to give it a surprising twist at the end!

★

What did the bear say to her mate?
"Not this winter, I have a headache!"

★

Why did the nymphomaniac go to the Indian reservation?
They offered her forty bucks!

★

Why should you wrap a gerbil in duct tape?
So it won't burst when you fuck it!

★

What would you call an R.N. who works in a massage parlor?
A pricktickle nurse!

★

Why are women like pianos?
When they're not upright, they're grand!

★

What's the newest movie about sea gulls?
Jonathan Livingston Sequel!

What do they sing to the guest of honor at a Fire Island banquet?
"For he gives jolly good fellatio . . ."

★

What's 71?
69 in the back seat with the couple in the front seat watching!

★

What would you call a female private eye?
A Dickless Tracy!

★

What's the definition of a meat grinder?
A snaggle-toothed sissy with the hiccups!

★

How do you get a cannibal cocktail?
Ubangi on the bar!

★

Why shouldn't you cut suppositories in half?
They're supposed to be shoved up your ass whole!

★

What's the best part of Sex Education?
Boning up for finals!

★

What would you call an Irish hooker who's good in bed?
Tramp O' Leen!

Why did the man on the flying trapeze want a divorce?
Because he was always catching his wife in the act!

What's another name for a virgin squaw?
A wouldn't Indian!

Why did the Polish girl think that there was something wrong with her birth control pills?
They kept falling out!

What would you call a drunk who's making love to an ugly girl?
High on the hog!

What happened to the Jewish nudist who got a hard-on and walked into a wall?
He broke his nose!

When do you know you've been married too long?
When what was once ideal is now ordeal!

How did Helen Keller's parents punish her?
By leaving the plunger in the toilet bowl!

What did the plumber say when the priest called up and said, "I've got a leak in my sink?"
"Go ahead! It's your sink!"

What's the speed limit on Highway 69?
Lickety-split!

What's blue and comes in brownies?
Cub Scouts!

What happened to the loser's loser?
His hand got pregnant!

Why wasn't the Polish couple upset when their infant son swallowed the prophylactic they had on the bed?
Because they had another one!

What's the worst thing about being caught in traffic?
You can hear what the hitchhikers are saying about you!

How late do college kids drink beer?
Until the wee-wee hours of the morning!

What's the coldest part of a man's body?
His testicles: two below!

What did one lesbian say to the other lesbian?
"Let's tie one on!"

What's a box spring?
An I.U.D.!

When do you call your wife Crisco?
When she's fat in the can!

Why are the newlywed Greek couple getting along so well?
Because she's bending over backwards to please him!

What happens if a girl doesn't wear undies in the winter?
She gets chapped lips!

Why did the girl on the dance floor get two inches taller
every time her partner twirled her around?
He was unscrewing her wooden leg!

What do you have if you use Kaopectate, Clearasil and birth
control pills?
No runs, no zits, no errors!

★

What's the difference between California and Florida?
In California, the *fruits* pick *you*!

★

Why did the scientist cross a gorilla with a porcupine?
He was trying to get a seat on the bus!

Why should you think twice before you make love to a girl doggie-style?
You might get hung up on her!

★

Why did the cop put soap in his unfaithful wife's Vaseline?
So she'd come clean!

★

What happens when an exhibitionist throws a party?
He goes all out!

★

How can you tell if a mosquito is Polish?
It bites Dolly Parton on the arm!

★

What's the difference between a hold-up and a stick-up?
Old age!

★

What do you catch from rubbing noses with an Eskimo girl?
Sniffilis!

★

Why do Madison Avenue executives walk around with their flies open?
Because they know it pays to advertise!

★

Why did the groom call room service and order lettuce for his new bride?
To see if she ate like a rabbit, too!

28

Why did the Polack take down the mirror over his bed?
He couldn't get used to shaving on his back!

★

What happened when they found a crack in the Statue of Liberty?
The Jolly Green Giant changed his vacation plans!

★

What's a kosher canoe?
Doesn't tip!

★

Where should you keep your jokes about oral sex?
On the tip of your tongue!

★

Why did the middle-aged couple go to bed early?
Something unexpected came up!

★

How do you get Hawaiian music?
Pour pineapple juice over your baked beans!

★

Why is it smart to buy your date drinks and dinner?
Because there's a good chance the rest of the night will be on her!

★

What's the best thing to do on a rainy day?
Put on your rubbers and go to town!

What advice did the father give his son when he heard the kid was going to porno movies?
"Keep it under your hat!"

★

Is it really wonderful when you're married?
It's really wonderful whether you're married or not!

★

Why do inflatable dolls make lousy dates?
Because if you bite 'em on the ear, they fart and fly out the window!

★

Why should you be very careful parking?
Because accidents cause people!

★

Why did the gymnast punch a guy for kissing her?
He kissed her in the middle of a cartwheel!

★

Why didn't the high school girl want to get married?
She wanted to wait until she had some experience under her belt!

★

What's a southern jock strap?
A Dixie cup!

★

Why did the Polack put ice cubes up his nose?
To keep his lunch cold!

30

How do you make a fruit cordial?
Pat him on the ass!

What do you get when you cross a Black with an octopus?
An incredible shoeshine!

Why did the high school kid take his date to the graveyard?
To bury a stiff!

What is it in the spring air that causes girls to get pregnant?
Their legs!

What did the hedgehog say when he got down off the hairbrush?
"Everybody makes mistakes!"

Why did the newlyweds leave the reception early?
To go get their things together!

What's the worst thing about performing for midgets?
You could get a standing ovation and not know it!

What should a girl do if she wants to see something swell?
Put her hand in a boy's lap!

31

Why didn't the nymphomaniac enjoy her date?
She just didn't have it in her!

Do girls get pimples around their periods?
No, mostly just on their faces and their asses!

How can you tell if your date is really into oral sex?
She pulls up her dress every time you yawn!

What do you get when you cross a donkey with an onion?
A piece of ass that sticks to the roof of your mouth!

How did they know the midget fell into the alphabet soup?
He sent up S.O.S.'s!

Why does Don Meredith have so many kids?
He uses Flow-through bags!

Why was the Orthodox Jew's wife frustrated?
He couldn't eat her because she was a pig!

How can you tell if somebody is a regular depositor at the
sperm bank?
He has a joint account!

Why was the gay company president smiling?
His right-hand man was up for a raise!

What did Dirty Johnny say to his mother when she stepped out of the shower?
"Well, Ma, how old were you when you wore it off?"

What has long hair and purple feet?
A lion that makes its own wine!

How many men suffer from wet dreams?
Nobody *suffers* from wet dreams!

What's wrinkled and hangs out your underwear?
Your mother!

What did the blind man say as he walked past the fish market?
"Good morning, ladies!"

What would you call a well-hung bear?
Genital Ben!

What would you call a Mexican gigolo?
Juan For the Money!

33

What's a pessimist?
A married optimist!

What would Michael Jackson be if he had a sex change?
A boy!

What's more macho than playing tackle football naked?
Playing *flag* football naked!

Why did the midget leave the nudist colony?
Because everyone looked like Fidel Castro!

What do you call Bloomingdale's on a day when all the gay
salesmen are home sick?
Deserted!

What would you call a Mexican with a vasectomy?
A dry Martinez!

What's the best thing about being a husband?
You get to screw the boss!

What's the new cologne for Blacks?
Eau de Doo-da-day!

What's the difference between a porcupine and a Porsche?
The porcupine has the pricks on the outside!

How do you know if a girl is really agile?
She can pull out her Tampax with her teeth!

What do you call it when a hooker has gas?
A prosti-toot!

Why are rabbis such a menace on the highway?
Because they're always cutting somebody off!

What's a good indication that your wife is not being faithful?
When the neighborhood kids set up their lemonade stands outside your bedroom!

Why do convicts love Hershey bars?
Because chocolate makes them break out!

What do you get when you cross Don Quixote and Dick Tracy?
Don Qui Dick!

What's better than an old broad with the bloom of youth in her cheeks?
An old broad with the cheeks of youth in her bloomers!

What should you ask a couple after they've announced their engagement?
"Which came first—the ring or the finger?"

How can you tell if your date is hard to satisfy?
If after sex she wants a Camel!

How fast can a girl go when she's having sex?
68 . . . If she went 69, she'd blow a rod!

Why did the nuclear physicist have so much trouble getting dates?
His breath had a half-life!

What can a girl put behind her ears to make her look sexy?
Her knees!

What kind of dungarees do lesbians wear?
Billie Jeans!

When should you start playing with yourself in a restaurant?
When there's a sign that says "First come, first served!"

Why couldn't the girl on the witness stand tell the judge what her assailant looked like?
Because she had been sitting on his face most of the time!

36

What would you call a Hungarian rowboat?
A hunky dory!

★

What's the sex change theme song?
Yes, We Have No Bananas!

★

How do you get a nun pregnant?
Fuck her!

★

Why did the priest get AIDS?
He forgot to clean his organ between hymns!

★

Why did the girl take a bath in peroxide?
Because she heard that on the whole gentlemen prefer blondes!

★

Why don't Polacks buy chewing tobacco?
Every time they try to light it they burn their mouths!

★

What's a kosher cold cut?
A Jewish American Princess breaking wind in the winter!

★

What would you call a girl who's fat and perverted?
A bisexual built for two!

How does Popeye keep his favorite tool from rusting?
He puts it in Olive Oyl!

What would you call the bouncer at a gay bar?
A flame thrower!

What's better than having a tiger in your tank?
Having a lady lyin' in your back seat!

How many Catholics does it take to plan a trip to Israel?
Two. One to ask "where?" and one to ask "why?"

What would a comedian rather do than make a girl crack up?
Feel her crack up!

★

Why are male private eyes better than female private eyes?
Because female private eyes wind up blowing too many assignments!

★

What happens when you're feeling low?
Your date slaps you!

★

Why does the Easter Bunny hide eggs?
He doesn't want anyone to know that he's been banging chickens!

What has a thousand teeth and eats wienies?
A zipper!

★

What should you do if you drop a quarter on Fire Island?
Kick it to Jones Beach before you pick it up!

★

What do you do if a baby cries?
Give it a bust in the mouth!

★

What is French asthma?
You can only catch your breath in snatches!

★

What's a loud wet dream?
A snorgasm!

★

What does a Black Jew say?
"Gimme five . . . percent!"

★

Why did the husband suddenly start suffering from premature ejaculation?
His wife reached for the contraceptive foam and accidentally grabbed the Easy-Off!

★

What did the lady cabbie say to the tourist who wanted to go to New York City's cheapest whorehouse?
"You're in it!"

39

What would you call a Frenchman who's had a vasectomy?
Monsieur Le Blanc!

★

What should you do if you go on a date with a telephone
operator and she won't give you the time of day?
Go home, put yourself on hold, and let your fingers do the
walking!

★

What's the biggest advantage of being a flasher?
You don't have to hold out your hand to see if it's raining!

★

Is it O.K. for a little girl to play with jacks?
Yes, as long as she also plays with eddie's, and bill's, and
charlie's . . .

★

What did the comic say as he fucked the fat girl?
"I'm on a roll!"

★

Why was Ronald McDonald fired?
For trying to stick his Big Mac into Wendy's hot and juicy!

★

What did the surgeon say to the guy who wanted to do his
own operation?
"Suture self!"

★

Which girls give the best head?
The ones that were breast-fed in a disco!

How can you tell which is the Greek schoolboy?
He's the one buttering up the teacher!

What's African roulette?
You go to bed with six native girls and one of them is a cannibal!

Why is Valentine's Day the horniest holiday?
Because everybody has a heart on!

What would you call a golf tournament for exhibitionists?
The Zipper Open!

Why didn't the Lone Ranger have any children?
He always went off in a cloud of dust!
(And all he shot were silver bullets!)

What do you do if you have a giraffe with three balls?
Walk him and pitch to the elephant!

★

How do you know if your relationship is liberated?
If you arm wrestle to see who has to sleep on the wet spot!

★

What's worse than a paper cut on your pecker?
A clamp on your clit! (Compare with a friend!)

How can you tell if a male stripper is really sexy?
The girls give him a standing ovulation!

★

What goes, "click, click, click, did I get it? . . . click, click, click, did I get it?"
Ray Charles trying to solve Rubik's Cube!

★

Why did the new bride slide down the banister?
To warm up her husband's dinner!

★

Why do the New York City gays want to put all the women in the Holland Tunnel and seal the ends?
So that the men will have to use the ferries!

★

If one mate is a spouse, what's more than one?
Spice!

★

Why didn't we celebrate at the end of the gas war?
Because gas won!

★

What would you call a Chinese porno star?
Dragon Willie!

★

Why don't nymphomaniacs ever vote?
They're too busy working around the poles!

42

How could you tell the two maggots were really horny?
They were making love in dead earnest!

Why is a sun-tanned girl like a roast chicken?
Because the white parts are the best!

Why is sex spelled s-e-x?
They couldn't spell Uh! Ooh! Ahhhh! Ooooohh!
Ahhuhuhah! Uhhh!

What did the fat nun say when her bra strap broke?
"My cup runneth over!"

What's the difference between a genealogist and a gynecologist?
A genealogist looks up your family tree, but a gynecologist
just peeks inside your bush!

What did the lady say when her husband announced that he
was going to become a necrophiliac?
"Over my dead body!"

What happens if you make love on a water bed?
You have a little squirt!

Why was the transvestite arrested?
Male fraud!

What folk singer would Orson Welles like to eat?
Buffet Sainte-Marie!

How can you tell if a golfer is nearsighted?
He's the one driving his caddy's nuts!

Why should you always travel with a six-pack in the winter?
In case you have to leave a message in the snow!

What did the tooth fairy bring Erik Estrada?
A plastic quarter!

What's the difference between a fox and a pig?
About six beers!

How do you know when your date is tired?
She can hardly keep her mouth open!

What's the feminine social disease called "Nixon's Afflic-
tion?"
Bugs in your oval office!

What's white and goes up?
A retarded snowflake!

How do you cut off a cat's tail?
Repossess his Cadillac!

What happened to the romantic who was mooning over a lost relationship?
He was arrested for indecent exposure!

Why should you be good to your friends?
Because without them, you'd be a total stranger!

Why is a woman like a screen door?
The more you bang 'em, the looser they get!

Why is there a cock on the weather vane?
Because if there was a pussy, the wind would blow right through it!

Why was the substitute teacher cross-eyed?
She couldn't control her pupils!

What did the flasher say to the Anheiser-Busch salesman?
"This pud's for you!"

What did the Catholic priest do when he saw Jesus Christ himself walking down the street?
Tried to look busy!

45

What's smaller than a flea's asshole?
Flea shit!

★

What's 137?
69 in the back seat, with the guy in the front seat getting blown while he watches the picture!

★

What would you call a girl who sleeps with every member of an orchestra?
A symphomaniac!

★

What did the teacher say when one of her students complained of diarrhea?
"Can that loose talk!"

★

What did one little old lady say to the other little old lady in the market?
"Let's go bananas!"

★

What does an Italian substitute teacher cook?
Spaghetti and spitballs!

★

What did the prudish girl do after her boyfriend kissed her on the cheek?
Pulled up her pants and ran into the house!

★

What do you find at the bottom of girls' undies?
Clitty litter!

What did the Indian say to the mermaid?
"How?"

★

What's a gay astronaut's greatest ambition?
To visit Uranus!

★

What's the difference between mono and herpes?
You get mono from snatching a kiss!

★

What would you call a girl who comes out of her face-lift surgery with no arms or legs?
Sue!

★

What does a gay waiter live for?
Tips!

★

What would you call a virgin on a water bed?
A cherry float!

★

What would you call a cow with five legs?
A bull!

★

Why are men like toilets?
Because they're either taken or they're full of shit!

What's the harshest penalty for bigamy?
Two mothers-in-law!

Why did they have to rush Gracie Allen to the hospital?
She had Burns between her legs!

Why should you never take a fourteen-year-old girl on your
water bed with you?
You could get in a raft of trouble!

What's a Fire Island bisexual?
A guy who likes both men and boys!

How do you make Paul Masson wine?
Squeeze his balls!

Why is a woman like a stamp?
Because you lick 'em, stick 'em, and send them on their
way!

What do you call a donkey thief?
An ass swiper!

Why do dykes like to work construction?
Because their Thermoses can double as dildoes!

How do you celebrate National Bird Week?
Give the person next to you a goose!

★

What would you call a drink made out of orange juice and milk of magnesia?
A Phillips Screwdriver!

★

What's the best way to make yourself last with your girlfriend?
Let everyone else go first!

★

What's six-foot-eight and picks lettuce?
A Maxican!

★

What's a "mourner?"
The same as a "nooner," only sooner!

★

Why did the politician staple his nuts together?
He figured if he couldn't lick 'em, he'd join 'em!

★

What do you do if you goose a girl and she yells, "Gross!"
Goose her 143 more times!

★

What did the beaver say to his date?
"It was nice gnawing you!"

What's next to the Andes?
The Amoses!

Why do they call them the "friendly skies of United?"
Because if you press a button a stewardess drops down on
your face!

What's a wool diaphragm?
A sock in the puss!

How can you tell a girl sardine from a boy sardine?
Watch which can they come out of!

What would George Washington be doing if he were alive
today?
Clawing on the inside of his coffin!

How can you tell if a Polack is on a computer date?
He's looking for a place to plug it in!

Why do carpenters get confused having sex?
Because they have to put their tool in the box when they
start, and take it out when they're done!

Why are squirrels like faggots?
Sometimes they have nuts in their mouths!

Do girls like paintings of nude men in their living rooms?
Yes, as long as they're hung well!

Why doesn't Rodney Dangerfield use the Yellow Pages?
Because every time he lets his fingers do the walking they
step in dog shit!

Why wasn't the macho man depressed that his lovemaking
partner didn't have an orgasm?
She told him he only missed by a couple of inches!

What's Liz Taylor's favorite game show?
Family Food!

How are all untalented contortionists alike?
They have trouble making ends meet!

What would you call a cock that flocks with French hens?
A blew bird!

What did the boss do when he heard that his secretary liked
to misbehave?
He chewed her out!

Why did Pia Zadora get thrown off the beach for wearing a
two-piece outfit?
It was a pair of socks!

What would you call gay groupies?
Band AIDS!

What's Dolly Parton's favorite candy?
Mounds!

What happened to the guy who invested his life savings in toilet paper and revolving doors?
He got wiped out before he could turn around!

What do you call it when a prostitute blows a midget in an alleyway?
A low trick!

Why is it weird making love with mirrors on all sides of the bed?
You feel like your date's asshole is spying on you!

What kind of car does Dr. Renee Richards drive?
A convertible!

How can you tell if a gangster is Polish?
His career is managed by three Black singers!

How do elephants make love underwater?
They take off their trunks!

What's green and slides down the hospital wall?
Mucus Welby!

★

How did the guy know that his wife was going to seek a divorce?
She bought towels that said "Hers" and "Hers Soon!"

★

What do you do if your nose goes on strike?
Picket!

★

What do you find under the hood in an Italian car?
His girlfriend!

★

What would you call a member of the Ku Klux Klan?
A sheethead!

★

How do you make paper dolls?
Screw an old bag!

★

What's a sanitary pad that girls can wear dancing?
Diskotex!

★

What would you call a sex change clinic on Long Island?
Cunts "R" Us!

Why do dogs lick themselves?
Because they can!
And they figure their reputations are shot from peeing on everything, anyway!

Why do Blacks' rear ends stick up?
Because when God asked the first Black what he wanted, he said, "Get my ass *high*!"

Why does a geologist walk around with his hands in his pockets?
He wants to leave no stone unturned!

What did the Polack do when he saw the sign over the motel toilet that said "Don't put anything but paper in this bowl?"
He shit on the floor!

What comes after 69?
Mouthwash!

What did the WASP say when his wife asked him if he loved her still?
"I'd better!"

What does a gay Eskimo get?
Kool-AIDS!

What's a job an ugly girl can always get?
Test pilot in a broom factory!

What's a barroom?
An elephant farting in an open elevator shaft.
(BARRROOOMM!!!)

Why does Liz Taylor keep chocolates around the house?
So she can snack between bites!

Why did the girl douche with Raid?
She was trying to get the bugs out of her sex life!

Why should a girl leave her blouse on if she falls overboard?
Because air gets in it and acts like a buoy!

What's a virgin at an orgy?
A newcomer!

Why are Greeks apathetic?
They're always indifferent!

★

Why did the hippie wash down his LSD with milk of magnesia?
He figured this trip he'd know where he was going!

Why are erections like elections?
It can get really sticky around the polls!

★

How do you get even with the guy who's trying to steal your wife?
Let him have her!

★

What should you do if you need acupuncture and can't afford it?
Start dating a porcupine!

★

Where do they keep golden beans?
Fart Knox!

★

What did the Italian kid do when his date told him to bring protection?
Brought his two brothers with him!

★

Why did the couple sleep back to back?
So they'd see eye to eye!

★

When does a cruel man beat his wife?
Every time!

★

What do you call a gay who doesn't have a boyfriend?
Free lance!

56

What's the difference between a peeping tom and a pickpocket?
A pickpocket snatches watches!

★

Why shouldn't you take a fat Italian girl on the dance floor?
You might get bumped off!

★

How can you tell if a Boy Scout is horny?
He's the one doing pushups over gopher holes when he's not eating Brownies!

★

What did the lady say when she heard that her husband had donated his penis to science?
"It's no big thing!"

★

When is a porcupine horny?
When she goes into prickly heat!

★

Why was the Mona Lisa smiling?
Leonardo da Vinci's fly was open!

★

What did the judge say to DeLorean when he caught him snorting cocaine in the Supreme Court men's room?
"John, this is the last straw!"

★

What's a fellow's first indication that he might be gay?
When sex on the whole doesn't interest him!

The biggest song hit of 1957 was . . .
(Check one)

_____ 1. *If I Had It To Do All Over, I'd Do It All Over You*
_____ 2. *She Was Only The Telegrapher's Daughter, But She Did It, Did It, Did It . . .*
_____ 3. *Legs Are A Girl's Best Friend, But Even The Best Of Friends Must Soon Part*
_____ 4. *I Was Painting My Girlfriend In The Nude, But Her Mother Came In And Made Me Put My Bathrobe On*
_____ 5. *I Never Saw A Dream Walking, But Once I Saw A Wet Dream Run*

★

What was the most tasteless bumper sticker of 1966?
(Cheque un)

_____ 1. "Teachers Do It With Class"
_____ 2. "I Honk When I Hit An Animal"
_____ 3. "Don't Honk If I'm Polish"
_____ 4. "Kamikazes Do It Once"
_____ 5. "Rugby Players Do It With Oddly-Shaped Balls"
_____ 6. "Practice Makes Pregnant"
_____ 7. "Vote For Horizontal Phone Booths"

★

When do you know you're incredibly horny?
(Stop checking off!)

_____ 1. You have to get it out before it turns to cheese.
_____ 2. You put a mirror over your bed so you can watch yourself beat off lefty.
_____ 3. You put a frog in your bathwater.
_____ 4. You visit your friends and they hide the Cheerios.
_____ 5. You want to find a gynecologist and talk shop.
_____ 6. You drill holes in the soap.

★

What's the height of conceit?
(Put your ego in check)

_____ 1. A flea floating down the river on his back, whistling for the drawbridge to open
_____ 2. Vanity license plates that say "Who Else?"
_____ 3. 5'11"
_____ 4. The Young Rascals's unreleased final album
_____ 5. Screaming your own name during orgasm

Find The Answer Across The Page!

_____ 1. What would you call a Polack who works at the post office?

_____ 2. What's brown and squishy and sticks between an elephant's toes?

_____ 3. Why are Polish stewardesses always so tired?

_____ 4. Why did the Polack sell his water skis?

_____ 5. Why aren't there any Polish druggists?

_____ 6. Why do Polacks have such nice noses?

_____ 7. Why can't Poland field a decent ice hockey team?

_____ 8. Why did the Polack take a leak on the park bench?

_____ 9. Why don't Polacks hunt elephants?

_____10. Why don't Polish women breast feed their babies?

_____11. How do you know the Polack at the airport?

_____12. Why don't Polacks eat dill pickles?

_____13. What's a Polish car pool?

_____14. Why did the Polish helicopter crash?

_____15. Why don't Polacks eat M&M's?

_____16. Why did the Polack sign up for night school?

_____17. How can you tell the Polish airplane in a snowstorm?

a. Wave to him!
b. Everybody drowns in spring training!
c. He's the one throwing bread to the planes!
d. It's the one with the hair under the wings!
e. Overqualified!
f. They meet at work!
g. From running alongside the planes holding up pictures of clouds!
h. They're hand-picked!
i. They're too tough to peel!
j. Because it said "Wet Paint!"
k. It got chilly, so the pilot turned off the fan!
l. They can't get their heads in the jars!
m. They can't get the little bottles in the typewriter!
n. The decoys are too heavy!
o. E-I-E-I-O!
p. He couldn't find a lake on a hill!
q. It hurts too much to boil their nipples!
r. He thought he was going to learn to read in the dark!
s. Slow natives!
t. So the rest of the team won't get horny!

On the honeymoon, the groom realizes that he has married a very fat girl when . . .
(Cheeeeeck all you want)

_____ 1. she walks out on the motel diving board and it lowers her into the pool.
_____ 2. he takes her to a ball game and the vendors all flip to see who gets their section.
_____ 3. she falls off the bed and rocks herself to sleep trying to get back up.
_____ 4. she needs binoculars to window-shop.
_____ 5. he takes her to a fancy boutique, and the only thing she can fit into is the awning!
_____ 6. she jumps into the ocean and bingo! It's high tide.
_____ 7. she doesn't have to put the toilet seat down when she takes a leak.
_____ 8. she stands in front of him naked and he can't see her pubic hair.
_____ 9. he doesn't know whether to fuck her or take the burro ride down.
_____10. at Mount Rushmore she can't decide which face to sit on.
_____11. her vibrator hums *East Side, West Side.*

★

What is the most popular expression for male homosexual?
(Check in the front)

_____ 1. Swishes
_____ 2. Dick-diet dannies
_____ 3. Meat smokers
_____ 4. Tearasses
_____ 5. Cocksuckers
_____ 6. Manure skewers
_____ 7. Head hunters
_____ 8. Brother fuckers
_____ 9. Sidesaddle tenors

What takes five minutes and lasts nine months?
(Check it out, check it out)

_____ 1. College registration
_____ 2. Johnson's Wax
_____ 3. Saying the wrong thing to your mother
_____ 4. Changing the batteries in your vibrator
_____ 5. There's one I think I left out; should I put it in?

★

The greatest lie of the twentieth century probably
will be . . .
(Check off less as you get older)

_____ 1. "Our layover time will be brief."
_____ 2. "One size fits all."
_____ 3. "I won't come in the mail."
_____ 4. "The check is in your mouth."
_____ 5. "My vasectomy left no scar."

★

What's the best indication that your date is
intellectual?
(Checque won)

_____ 1. She can listen to *The William Tell Overture* and
not think about The Lone Ranger.
_____ 2. She can say "headache" in four languages.
_____ 3. She has no tits whatsoever.
_____ 4. She says "prophylactic" instead of "bag."
_____ 5. She enjoys doing the Rorschach test with the wet
spot.

63

The most popular "obvious yes" answer of the fifties was . . .
(Checky Chubber)

_____ 1. "Is a pig's ass pork?"
_____ 2. "Did Noah have wet dreams?"
_____ 3. "Does an old dog fart?"
_____ 4. "Do grandmas give gummers?"
_____ 5. "Does a proctologist use a rear-view mirror?"
_____ 6. "Is a four-pound robin fat?"

★

When do you know your penis is too small?
(Write in any and all tips)

_____ 1. When you put it in your date's hand and she says, "You know I don't get high."
_____ 2. When you have to shoot where other men reach
_____ 3. When you realize that if you got circumcised again you'd have a scab on your ass
_____ 4. When you put your jock on backwards and it fits
_____ 5. When you have to fold it in half and go for thickness
_____ 6. When you accidentally pull out a hair and piss down your leg
_____ 7. When you have to sprinkle it with black pepper and catch it when it comes out to sneeze
_____ 8. When a cop sees you streaking and feels so sorry for you that he gives you two free tickets to the Policemen's Ball
_____ 9. When you're fucking a girl the best you can and she tells you to start any time
_____10. When you go through a trial marriage and you're convicted
_____11. When your girlfriend feeds you hot dog helper
_____12. When you realize you couldn't gag a maggot
_____13. When you're on the high school football team and the coach never plays you, but makes you take a shower anyway, claiming that it's "good for the team's morale"

II.

What does a dog do that a man steps into??
Pants!!!

What's a smartass?
Someone who can sit on an ice-cream cone and tell you what flavor it is!

★

What's the best way to come first in a woman's thoughts?
Be sure to let her come first in bed!

★

What would you call a sanitary napkin for girls with bald crotches?
Kojax!

★

When is premature ejaculation a serious problem?
When it occurs between "hello" and "what's your sign?"

★

What happened to the couple that met through the social disease hot line?
They lived "herpily ever after!"

★

Why were the cops so mad that the toilet bowl was stolen from the police station?
They had nothing to go on!

★

How does a French politician campaign?
He travels around the country, kissing all the babies
. . . before they're born!

★

Why did the scoutmaster put shoe polish in his Vaseline?
So he could rise and shine!

How do Jews commit suicide?
They hang from the rafters with one hand and choke themselves with the other, to save the price of the rope!

What happens if you sit in wet cement?
You get hardening of the farteries!

Why was Willie Nelson hit by a car?
He was playing *On The Road Again!*

What's worse than pecker tracks on your zipper?
Zipper tracks on your pecker!

What does a gynecologist do when he's feeling sentimental?
Looks up an old girlfriend!

What's green and sings sincerely?
Frank Sinatt!

What's the last thing to go through a bug's mind after he hits your windshield?
His asshole!

Why do girl cheerleaders wear sexy outfits?
It makes the boys root harder!

68

What would you call a faggot in an insane asylum?
A swishkaboob!

★

What was Moby Dick's father's name?
Papa Boner!

★

Why did the Polack turn down a blowjob?
He had three weeks left on his unemployment!

★

How can you tell if a track star is gay?
He's always trying to lap the other runners!

★

What's the best thing to do if you're on a date with an annoying nymphomaniac?
Give her a vibrator and tell her to buzz off!

★

Why is sex so confusing?
Because you find so much loose stuff in tight pants!

★

Who's the horniest guy ever?
The guy that wanted his old room back a week after he was born!

★

What should you do if you're swallowed by a whale?
Run around until you get pooped out!

How can you tell if a transvestite is happy-go-lucky?
All he wants to do is eat, drink and be Mary!

Why are orgies in the woods so popular?
Because people come in groves!

How many Zen Buddhists does it take to change a light bulb?
Two. One to change it, and one to not change it!

What would you call a tired old gigolo?
Don Worn!

What would you call a song about Moon Zappa skinny-dipping during her period?
Red River Valley Girl!

What would you call a Scotch queer?
Ben Doon!
And his boyfriend?
Phil McCrevis!

What's the best way to stop the stork?
Shoot it in the air!

What two things most frequently cause unhappy marriages?
Men and women!

What do you call a lesbian who drives a delivery truck full of dildoes?
A dick van dyke!

★

What did the guy say when he started to suffer from premature ejaculation and diarrhea?
"Easy come, easy go!"

★

How can you tell if a cannibal is gay?
He always blows lunch!

★

How do you sink a Polish submarine?
Knock on the door!

★

Why did the gigolo park in the handicapped space?
He had chapped lips!

★

Why does a dog lift his leg to pee?
It shifts his ass out of gear so that he doesn't shit on his paws!

★

How can you tell if a skunk is nearsighted?
He's asking a fart for a date!

★

What would you call a nurse who gives midnight head?
Florence Nightengulp!

What would you call a nun who's had a sex change?
A transister!

How did the maid show her appreciation after the butler gave her a bottle of Scotch for Christmas?
She polished it off for him!

What do you use to make a pickle cake?
Dill dough!

Why do they cut the heads off sardines?
So they won't bite each other in the can!

How can you tell if a cowboy is gay?
He rides into town and shoots up the sheriff!

When has a nymphomaniac cheerleader reached her pinnacle?
When she's put in charge of halftime entertainment at the toilet bowl!

What do you do if your girlfriend catches you jerking off?
Tell her you were trying to jump-start her vibrator!

What would you call a sex change in Puerto Rico?
A hole in Juan!

72

What do you get when you cross a donkey with a gopher?
Assholes in your garden!

How can you tell if an Indian is gay?
All his scalps have handles!

Why should you put Vaseline in your cooking oil?
It keeps the meat from sticking!

What's the best kind of Jewish car accident?
No damage to the car and everyone inside is hurt!

What's worse than a piano that's out of tune?
An organ that stops working in the middle of a piece!

Why did the fag go drinking on St. Patty's day?
To get his Irish up!

Why did the college kid keep pouring shots of booze on his hand?
He was trying to get his date drunk!

Why should you never let your girlfriend chase you in church?
She might catch you by the organ!

★

Why did the Polack walk around all day in a wet shirt?
Because it said "wash and wear!"

★

Why is Billie Jean King so popular?
Because the women just eat her up and no men are down on her!

★

Why do farts smell?
So deaf people can enjoy them, too!

★

What's worse than eating something you don't want to?
Waking up being fed something you didn't order!

★

When do you know you're really bowlegged?
When you can get out of both sides of bed at the same time!

★

Why did the Black guy wear a tuxedo to his vasectomy?
He figured if he was gonna *be* impotent, he was gonna *look* impotent!

★

Why did the girl fail Sex Education?
She couldn't come for the oral exam!

74

What should a couple do if they want to go steady?
Buy a case of Ex-Lax!

★

Why is it easy to find Dolly Parton's Homemade Wine on the shelves?
It's in the biggest jugs!

★

What's a Cherokee gigolo?
A high-performance Injun!

★

What's the only thing to do if you have an orgasm every time you sneeze?
Sniff black pepper!

★

What would you call a Jewish faggot?
Heblew!

★

What did the Polish girl say when the dog licked her belly?
"Down, boy!"

★

What's worse than drinking Mexican water?
Drinking Mexican prune juice!

★

Who wears pink tights and drives a chariot?
Ben Gay!

What does everyone yell when Orson Welles walks into Burger King?
"The Whopper's home!"

★

Who was the first black prostitute?
Renta Kuntay!

★

How many straight New York City waiters does it take to change a light bulb?
Both of them!

★

When does a guy know he's a good lover?
His date is bored to tears!

★

When does a toll collector know she's reached middle age?
When she starts going through her exact change of life!

★

Why was the girl hesitant to get engaged to the contortionist?
She was afraid he'd break it off!

★

What was Dolly Parton voted by her high school graduating class?
Cutest couple!

★

What's the shortest bedtime story?
"No!"

When do you know you have a serious gas problem?
When you fart in the bathtub and the bubbles sink!

What's the best thing to do when you're on a hot date?
Stay on her!

What do you call mouthwash for call girls?
Whoroscope!
What do you call mouthwash for dwarfs?
Microscope!
What do you call chocolate-flavored mouthwash?
Boscope!

Why is a fat girl like a moped?
They're both fun to ride until your friends see you!

Why did the French horn player's wife sue for divorce?
Because every time he kissed her he stuck his hand up her ass!

What should you do if an elephant comes in your window?
Swim!

What would you call a kosher sea captain?
Yom Skippur!

What should you do if your date yells, "I can't take it any longer!"?
Tell her not to worry; it's not gonna get any longer!

What weighs two thousand pounds, lives in the ocean, and
doesn't make house calls?
Moby Doc!

What's a bedside breath candy?
A predickamint!

Where's the best place to play water polo?
In a school of blowfish!

Why are sex manuals useless?
Because learning about sex from a book is like learning to
fly from a pigeon that got hit by a truck!

Who rode a chariot and every woman in Rome?
Ben Herpes!

What's artificial insemination?
A technical knock-up!

What do sharks eat for breakfast?
Bacon and legs!

Why couldn't Joan Collins be a cheerleader?
Every time she did a split, six high school rings fell out!

What would you call a roomful of Marines with boners?
The Hard Corps!

What's the difference between a good date and a great date?
A good date wants you to kiss her when she leasts expects it.
A great date wants you to kiss her *where* she least expects it!

Why do dogs like Christmas?
Because two weeks out of the year they have indoor plumbing!

When does a man flirt with another man?
When he wants to end up with him!

What's something Michael Jackson can't do to Billie Jean King?
Thriller!

Why was the Jewish gigolo banned from the all-night diner?
Because he had stiffed all the waitresses!

How did the horse get rich in New York City?
He made a pile on Wall Street!

What happens if you drink Ex-Lax with Spanish fly in it?
After two sips you don't know whether you're coming or going!

Why do Blacks keep chickens in their back yards?
To teach their children how to walk!

If you have V.D., what do you know for sure?
Urine trouble!

Why is it so much fun to go to a bar that has card games in the back room?
Because all night long it's liquor in the front and poker in the rear!

What's the best way to make crab cakes?
Start from scratch!

Why did the Polack make love to his sister?
He had it in for his brother-in-law!

What's the best part of a porno movie?
The coming attractions!

What's the one rule at an orgy?
To come with the person that brought you!

What should you do if your date won't make love with the lights on?
Close the car door!

How did Dolly Parton get two black eyes?
Jogging!

What would you call a gay who worked at a rug factory?
Fruit of the loom!

What do you call a guy who goes to a Saturday matinee and
sits alone in the balcony?
A tier jerker!

When do you know you have bad buckteeth?
When you can bob for apples without bending over!

What did one boob say to the other?
"We better stop hanging so low, they'll think we're nuts!"

What do you do if your girl tells you to "kiss her where it
smells?"
Drive her to New Jersey!

What would you call a ballplayer who beats up gays?
A swish hitter!

What would you call a Chinese Harvard student?
A pleppie!

81

What did the Indian say when the prostitute tied a knot in his pecker?
"How come?"

★

How did Adolph the Brown-Nosed Reindeer get his name?
He could run as fast as Rudolph, he just couldn't stop as fast!

★

How can you tell if a bride is anxious?
She comes walking down the aisle!

★

How can you tell if two faggots are intellectual?
They're blowing each other's minds!

★

What do dogs hate most about the winter?
Getting frozen to fire hydrants!

★

What happened to Linda Lovelace's grandmother?
She went down on the Titanic!

★

What comedian do you find in every elevator?
Red Buttons!

★

How does a Polack get his wife off?
He pushes her!

Why was Little Jack Horner sitting in the corner?
He was eating his pumpkin's pie!

★

What happens if a lady golfer gets hit with a golf ball
between the first and the second hole?
It doesn't leave a lot of room for the Band-Aid!

★

What's the difference between a Jewish girl and a toilet?
The toilet doesn't follow you around when you're done
using it!

★

Why would Kotex be effective as a national defense
product?
They would keep the Reds in, the Poles out, the Greeks
happy, and the French hungry!

★

Why is it stupid for a man to get a little bit on the side?
Because there's so much more around the front!

★

Why shouldn't you drink diet soda after oral sex?
Because then you have *two* aftertastes to get rid of!

★

How did the Polish feminist scar her chest?
She burned her bra without taking it off!

★

How do you get into a foxhole?
First, you lift up its tail!

How are homosexuals created?
Twenty-five percent are born and the rest are sucked into it!

Why did the Pillsbury Doughgirl get pregnant?
Because the Pillsbury Doughboy forgot his wiener wrap!

Which president wore the biggest rubbers?
The one with the biggest feet!

What did the sign on the whorehouse door say?
"Out To Lunch! Beat It!"

What do they call an abortion in Prague?
A canceled Czech!

Why did the Italians lose the war?
They ordered ziti instead of shells!

How do you know it's really raining hard?
The exhibitionists are out in Glad Bags!

What's the difference between a midget detective agency
and a ladies' track team?
A midget detective agency is a cunning bunch of runts!

Why did the girl put her date's dick in the waffle iron?
She wanted to make a lasting impression on him!

How many feminists does it take to change a light bulb?
That's not funny!

When do you know times are hard?
The hookers are swallowing!

What's the scariest thing about a Polish seafood restaurant?
They only serve clams on the half shell when the chefs have head colds! (When they're in sneezin'!)

How can you tell a boy pancake from a girl pancake?
By the way they're stacked!

Why doesn't Ronald Reagan take baths?
He wants to live to a ripe old age!

Why did the Polack run out of the girl's bedroom when he saw her diaphragm on her dresser?
He thought it was a prophylactic and didn't want to meet the monster that owned it!

Why didn't the Jewish guy report that his credit cards were stolen?
Because the thief was spending so much less than his wife!

How did the four guys carry the huge drunken fat girl out of the bar?
Two abreast!

85

Why didn't the cop get the nymphomaniac's name?
He figured it was a case of shoot first and ask questions later!

★

How do porcupines make love?
Very carefully!

★

When does your father really get annoyed at you picking pimples?
When they're on *his* face!

★

How can you tell if two truckers are gay?
They exchange loads!

★

Why did the Polack stick toothpicks in the baked beans?
To let the gas out!

★

What should a college boy do if a pretty girl that sits next to him in one of his classes misses a lecture?
Invite her up to his apartment and fill her in!

★

How can you tell if a motorcyclist is happy?
He has bugs in his, teeth!

★

When do you know your sex life is picking up?
When you can switch hands without missing a stroke!

What did the guy say after his girlfriend farted while he was going down on her?
"Ahh! A breath of fresh air!"

What did the psychiatrist say to the patient who was sensitive about the size of his penis?
"I wouldn't let a little thing like that bother you!"

What would you call a guy who can talk girls into letting him go down on them in five different languages?
A cunning linguist!

What's the difference between the first honeymoon and the second honeymoon?
On the second honeymoon, the *husband* sits on the edge of the bed crying, "It's too big!"

Why did the Italian empty his watch on his pizza?
He wanted it with the works!

How do you join a sex club?
It's easy! No dues, no meetings . . . just come!

What did one fly say to the other fly?
"Your human is open!"

Why do Donnie, Marie and all the Osmonds have diarrhea?
Runs in the family!

87

What would you call a French-African restaurant?
"Chez What!"

★

What's the best way for a golfer to hit his balls squarely?
Step on a rake!

★

What's a hamburger kiss?
Between the buns!

★

How can you tell the gay baby in the maternity ward?
He's the one with the pacifier in his ass!

★

What's the difference between "oooh" and "aahhh?"
About three inches!

★

When do you know your breath is really bad?
When you smoke a cigarette and blow onion rings!

★

Why did the guy trade his wife for a Datsun pickup?
It had a smaller box and a smoother ride!

★

Why did Wurlitzer merge with Xerox?
To make reproductive organs!

★

Why was the businessman depressed?
Because his business went bankrupt and the bottom fell out of his wife!

What does a Jewish American Princess do if she gets her period while she's on vacation?
Calls womb service!

What's the definition of "frenzy?"
Five hundred blind lesbians locked in a tuna fish factory!
What did they say when a guy wanted to come in?
"Sorry, Charlie!"

How can you tell if you're having a wild orgasm?
Your partner wakes up!

How do you know when you're really bowlegged?
They hang you over the door for good luck!

Why didn't the Polish sergeant worry about herpes?
He heard it was a disease of the privates!

What did Ronald Reagan say at the ballet?
"Why don't they just get taller girls?"

What did the rabbi say as he started to cut?
"It won't be long, now!"

How can you tell when you've arrived in San Francisco?
The mounted police are riding sidesaddle!

89

How can you tell if a nymphomaniac has been on a successful fishing trip with her boyfriend?
She comes home with a red snapper!

How can you tell a Polish blackjack dealer?
His shoes are off and his fly is open!

How can you tell if an Indian is gay?
He's a brave sucker!

What would you call a virgin cowgirl?
Hopalong Chastity!

What did the bug say after he splattered on the biker's forehead?
"If I had the guts, I'd do it again!"

How should you celebrate a vasectomy?
With a bottle of Dry Sac!

What's worse than a waitress who keeps hamburgers warm in her armpits?
A waitress who keeps the hot dogs warm!

Why did one faggot invite the other faggot to go out on his boat?
He was hoping he'd be taken up on it!

90

Do men prefer fat thighs or skinny thighs?
Somewhere in between!

★

How many feminists does it take to change a light bulb?
Three. One to change the bulb, one to write about the socket
being exploited and one to wish she was the socket!

★

Why is cocaine like cock?
Because once a girl has had some, she can't get enough of
it!

★

What does a maid do when she's horny?
Dusts herself off!

★

How can you tell the gay Jewish weight lifter?
He's the one in the locker room pumping Myron!

★

Why didn't the skeleton cross the road?
He didn't have the guts!

★

What's the difference between Queen Elizabeth and
Elizabeth Taylor, after sex?
Queen Elizabeth says, "Why didn't I, Philip?";
and Liz Taylor says, "Why didn't I fill up?"

★

How do you know it's been a wild date?
Stretch marks on your tongue!

91

What do you need to make it in business as a gigolo?
A very cooperative staff!

How does a couple find each other in the dark?
Wonderful!

What's the definition of a real dyke?
A lady that rolls her own tampons and can suck-start a
Harley Davidson!

What's the difference between "like" and "love?"
If a girl likes you, she'll let you.
If she loves you, she'll help you!

What's the *real* difference between "like" and "love?"
The difference between spit and swallow!

Why did the old maid call in an electrician?
She got tired of using candles!

How do you make an elephant fly?
You start with a huge zipper!

How can you tell diarrhea is hereditary?
It runs in your genes!

92

Why did the gigolo's business fall off?
He had leprosy!

Why does a Polish girl close her eyes when she's fucking?
So she can fantasize that she's masturbating!

What did the jock say to the family jewels?
"Hang in there. I won't let you down!"

When should you eat refried beans?
When you want to get your second wind!

What can a girl do to keep from getting pregnant?
Nothing!

Where did the two crabs fall in love?
The Policeman's Ball!

Why did the train full of lumber coming into the U.S. from
Canada stop in Buffalo?
To let the lumberjack off!

What did the determined girl say on the way to her first
gymnastics class?
"I'm gonna learn to stand on my head or bust!"

What does AIDS stand for?
Another Infested Dick Smoker
(or, "Ass Is Diseased, Sorry!")

What did the grape say when the elephant sat on it?
Nothing. It just let out a little wine!

Why do female paratroopers wear heavy-duty undies?
So they won't whistle on the way down!

Why did the faggot freak out when he got the mumps?
He thought that he was pregnant!

If a guy busts his left hand, how's his sex life?
All right!

What did the farmer say when he caught the hired hand with
his wife?
"You might want to plug your ears, too. This gun is mighty
loud!"

What do you call it when a midget gets circumcised?
Tiny trim!

How do you win the prize at the synagogue bazaar?
Guess the number of foreskins in the mayonnaise jar!

What's another name for an orgy?
Grope therapy!

What crawls and goes "ding dong?"
A wounded Avon lady!

What do you get when you cross a rooster with a peanut butter sandwich?
A cock that sticks to the roof of your mouth!

What did the two sisters say after they returned from the sex change clinic as brothers?
"Look, Ma, no cavities!"

How can you tell the urologist in the men's room?
He's the one that washes his hands *before* he takes a leak!

What would you call an Indian with three testicles?
A buck and a half!

What did the horny lion tamer say to the lion?
"I'm just gonna put my head in!"

When does a girl consider her complexion to be a problem?
When she has to take off her make-up with an ice-cream scoop!

★

What did the Polack in the police lineup say when they brought in the victim?
"That's her!"

★

What do you get when you masturbate into the K-Y?
Penis butter and jelly!

★

How can you tell if your dog is loyal?
If he lifts his leg to your family tree!

★

What did the panties say to the poontang?
"Don't move a hair! I've got you covered!"

★

Why do they say that David Letterman has western teeth?
Because of all the wide open spaces!

★

What did the honeymoon couple do on the stalled elevator?
Got off between floors!

★

What's the advantage of dating a Ubangi?
You can get head without taking off your pants!

How can you tell if a bricklayer is Polish?
His pecker is worn!

Why don't doctors like to operate on obese women?
Because it's hard to balance the patients on them!

What's the worst thing about sleeping with a man who has
two penises?
Not knowing which end is up!

Why did the little boy want to get into the little girl's pants?
Because he'd shit in his!

How do you get to see the official bird of New York City?
Cut somebody off!

What's the cheapest entertainment you can get?
Serve beans at a hot-tub party!

What's the easiest way to get a little group sex?
Use both hands!

How do you know Adam was Polish?
He had Eve and the apple, and he ate the apple!

97

Is it wrong to have sex before you're married?
Only if it makes you late for the ceremony!

What's the ultimate practical joke?
Giving your nearsighted aunt a frog and telling her it's a green vibrator!

What would you call a gay fruit fly?
A faggot maggot!

What does an actor do when he forgets his lines?
Goes on stage straight!

What did one strawberry say to the other strawberry?
"If we hadn't been in that bed together, we wouldn't be in this jam!"

What would you call an Italian hooker with gas?
A pastatoot!

Why did the nymphomaniac only date nervous men?
So when they made love she could fantasize that it was her vibrator!

What lies under the table at the massage parlor with its tongue hanging out?
Your shoe!

What did the hooker say when the preacher told her to pick three hymns?
"Him, him and him!"

★

Why does an Indian wear a jock strap?
Totem pole!

★

What's black and white and hides in a cave?
A zebra that's behind on his alimony payments!

★

Why is sex like air?
Because it's no big thing unless you aren't getting any!

★

How can you tell if a golfer is an idiot?
He almost ruptures himself using the ball cleaner!

★

What would you call a girl who gets stoned all day and makes homemade rugs?
The Happy Hooker!

★

When should you stop masturbating?
When the smoke alarm goes off!

★

What weighs two thousand pounds and has a stick up its ass?
A hippopopsicle!

What's the definition of a "brute"?
A guy that puts on a prophylactic with a tire iron!

Why was the farmer suspicious of one of the hired hands?
Because his ass was as tan as his arms!

Why did Liz Taylor cross the road?
To get to the other thigh!

Why don't girls like to drink beer on the beach?
Because they get sand in their Schlitz!

What's better to wear, a sweatshirt or a windbreaker?
It depends on whether you're gonna sweat or break wind!

What does a taxidermist do when he gets horny?
Buries himself in his work!

What do you call shock absorbers in a compact car?
Passengers!

How can you tell if a termite is gay?
He only eats mailboxes!

What did one lesbian say to the other lesbian?
"Your face or mine?"

What did Ronald Reagan say after he first met Nancy and she told him that she was a nymphomaniac?
"I don't care if you steal, as long as you're true to me!"

★

What's the best thing to do after you've had it out with your girlfriend?
Put it back in!

★

When do you know you're really effeminate?
You *walk* with a lisp!

★

What would you call a Flugelhorn player who was really into video games?
Pac Mangione!

★

What would you call a whore's children?
Brothel sprouts!

★

What should you do if a girl tells you that the batteries in her vibrator are dead?
Jump her!

★

What's unique about the newly issued stamp that commemorates Gay Liberation?
It licks *you*!

★

How can you tell which horse is itchy?
He's the one with the buggy behind!

How did the girl who fell in the cesspool save herself?
She couldn't swim, but she went through all the movements!

Why was the Polack's penis transplant a failure?
His hand rejected it!

What's the difference between a rhinoceros and the Lawrence Welk Orchestra?
The rhinoceros has the horns in the front and the asshole in the back!

Why is sex better than bowling?
The balls are lighter and you don't have to change your shoes!

What do you call a brothel full of jaundiced prostitutes?
Whores of a different color!

★

Who's the meanest person in the world?
The guy who short-sheeted Mahatma Gandhi!

Why did so many Mexicans show up at the Alamo?
Because they heard that Davy Crockett was beating them off!

★

What do you get when you cross an anteater with a vibrator?
An armadildo!

102

How can you tell which street vendor is an exhibitionist?
He's the one with the hot dog wagon!

Why don't they teach karate to Polish Marines?
Too many saluting accidents!

What do you call the bread a cheap hooker gives her main man?
Pimpernickel!

Why did Miss Piggy miss her last concert?
She had a frog in her throat!

You eat apples, apples come out. You eat bananas, bananas come out. What should you do?
Eat shit!

What's brown and lays in the forest?
Smokey the Prostitute!

If the shrimps are coming in on the shrimp boats, how do the crabs come in?
On the captain's dinghy!

How does a New York City cabbie solve Rubik's Cube?
He drives over it!

What would you call a gay Mexican?
A señor eater!

Why don't exhibitionists retire?
They'd rather stick it out forever!

What did the zipper say to the foreskin?
"How's *that* grab you!?"

When's the worst time to pee in the pool?
When you're on the diving board!

Why do all gay men have moustaches?
To hide the stretch marks!

What's an elephant do on the highway?
About four miles an hour!

Why should a fool keep a cool tool?
Because she's wise to the rise in his Levi's!

Why does Pia Zadora have boyfriends by the score?
Because they all *do*!

Why doesn't God ever vacation on earth?
Because the last time he came down, about two thousand
years ago, he banged some Jewish girl and they're still
talking about it!

★

Who's the best-smelling prizefighter?
Deo Duran!

★

Why didn't the girl scream for help when she was molested?
Her parents taught her never to talk with her mouth full!

★

What did the sea gull say as it flew over the Kentucky
Derby?
"I'm gonna put everything I've got on Number Seven!"

★

What did the plastic surgeon do when he got depressed
about his penis size?
He hung himself!

★

What did the wife say when she found her husband in bed
with a lady midget?
"At least he's tapering off!"

What does every Black rabbi say?
"Gimme some skin!"

Why do girls wear tight sweaters?
To make mountains out of molehills!

When do you know you have a *very* serious gas problem?
The Dutch government tries to import you to jump-start
windmills!

What's the difference between a dog lying in the road and
Howard Cosell lying in the road?
There are skid marks in front of the dog!

What goes in hard and pink and comes out soft and sticky?
Bubble gum!

When should you wear *two* rubbers?
When it's raining!

What's the difference between a frog and a horny toad?
A frog goes, "Ribit, ribit," and a horny toad goes, "Rub it,
rub it!"

★

How did John DeLorean get plowed under?
He tried to move a lot of snow and the government caught
his drift.

★

What's the best hand in strip poker?
A royal flash!

★

How do you make holy water?
Take some water and boil the hell out of it!

Why did the rooster cross the basketball court?
He heard the referee was blowing fouls!

★

What's Pia Zadora's favorite four-letter word?
"Next!"

★

Who was the first bookkeeper?
Adam. He turned over a leaf and made an entry!

★

What's the definition of a "nice Greek boy?"
A Greek boy that takes a girl out twice before he sleeps with
her brother!

★

Why is marriage like a cafeteria?
Because you take what you want and pay for it later!

★

What's the difference between "picnic" and "panic?"
About thirty days!

★

What's the difference between frustration and panic?
Frustration is the first time you find out you can't do it the
second time, and panic is the second time you find out you
can't do it the first time!

★

How do you make a handkerchief dance?
Put a little boogie in it!

107

Why does an elephant have four feet?
He'd look pretty silly with six inches!

Why did the girl put beans in her boyfriend's birthday cake?
So it would blow out its own candles!

What would you call a sex change surgeon?
A gender amender!

Why are edible underwear so popular?
Because so many girls are stuck on them!

How can you tell if you're in a gay bar?
They shake hands with you while your hand is still in your pocket!

How do you keep an elephant from stampeding?
Cut off his stampeder!

What does a mathematician do if he's constipated?
Works it out with a pencil!

Where does a proctology student go?
To the rear of his class!

Who gets physical and sells cocaine?
Bolivia Newton-John!

What happens if you don't pull out in time?
You get a parking ticket!

What would you call an all-night Chinese restaurant?
Wok Around the Clock!

What would happen if the Mafia merged with the Gay
Liberation Front?
The kiss of death would come with dinner and dancing!

How do you customize a bicycle for a gay?
Take off the seat!

What's a virgin apple?
One that's never had a worm in it!

What happens if you moon in bumper-to-bumper traffic?
You wind up with your ass in a jam!

What did the Elephant Man say to Eleanor Roosevelt?
"Now I *know* I'm not an animal!"

Why do Jewish guys get circumcised?
Because Jewish girls like *anything* that's twenty-five percent off!

What do they serve on the middle floor of the Statue of Liberty?
A box lunch!

What's better than masturbating with people watching?
Masturbating with people watching who don't know you're doing it!

Why did Dirty Johnny think that his father was gay?
Because his father was always talking about "chewing out the prick next door!"

What's a male octopus called?
An octocock!

What happened to the Indian who drank one hundred gallons of tea?
They found him drowned in his tea pee!

How was copper wire invented?
Two Jews fighting over a penny!

What's the only way an India rubber man can get girls?
On the rebound!

When do you call a plumber and a hooker?
When you want to get your pipes cleaned while you're getting your pipes cleaned!

★

What's brown, sugar-coated, and runs around holding its side?
A gingerbread man with a hernia!

★

What would you call a gay wino?
A grapefruit!

★

Why can't Mary Kay walk very fast?
Her lipstick!

★

Why did the housewife stay in bed when the salesman came to the door?
She was prone to fool around!

★

When do you know you've had the world's best head?
You have to pull the sheets out of your ass!
When do you know you have the world's best woman?
She does that for you, too!

★

How does a girl like to have her tummy tickled?
From the inside!

111

How are the marriage proposals of today different from the marriage proposals of the past?
In the past, when a man proposed, *he* was the one on his knees!

★

What's a cynical Jew's motto?
"L'chaim doesn't pay!"

★

What did Emily Post say to her husband when he got a boner?
"It's not polite to point!"

★

How does a couple with hemorrhoids pass the time?
Some nights they put in each other's Preparation H, and some nights they just sit and watch the tube!

★

How do you know when there's a pervert on your flight?
The stewardesses have to tell him to buckle up on his way back from the lavatory!

★

What happens when a rabbi puts a screen in your foreskin?
You get a filter tip!

★

What's one thing that New York City tourists agree on?
Parking is such sweet sorrow!

★

What do you call a pecker in a knot?
A Willie Nelson!

112

Why did the Fire Island pickpocket keep coming up empty-handed?
He was just browsing!

★

What's the difference between sin and shame?
It's a sin to put it in; it's a shame to take it out!

★

Why shouldn't you ever kiss a girl's ass?
Because you'll get a crack in the jaw!

★

When is it silly to have Grandma for dinner?
When you still have half of Aunt Peg in the freezer!

★

What do you call a Jewish girl's nipples?
The tips of the iceberg!

★

When do you know you're really enjoying a porno movie?
When you butter your own popcorn!

★

Why did the nymphomaniac fail her road test?
The car stalled, and from force of habit she jumped into the back seat!

★

How does a humorous gynecologist greet his patients?
"At your cervix!"

What's the difference between a rooster and a lawyer?
A rooster clucks defiance!

When is a Jewish American Princess good in bed?
When she's trying to dry her toenail polish!

What's the first thing you see when you walk into a topless restaurant?
Hostess twinkies!

Why couldn't the cop arrest the bar owner who was going down on a girl in the window of his club?
He had a liquor license!

Why shouldn't a girl marry a guy who's good and ready?
Because by the time a guy's ready, he's not any good!

What's the hardest thing about the sex change from a man to a woman?
Inserting the anchovies!

What did the Jewish man say when his wife asked him to diet?
"Vat color vould you like it?"

How do the literary snobs view joke books like this one?
As pubic hair in the teeth of life!

What did the dentist get when he crossed his nurse's nooky with nitrous oxide?
Laughing gash!

What does Miss Piggy douche with?
Hogwash!

What happens to boys that lie?
They get girls!

What cake mix do homosexuals use?
Dunkin' Heinies!

Why do girls use perfumed genital spray?
It gives their sex mouth appeal!

Where's the best place to be when a woman winks at you?
Under the table!

What did the lady say to the midget at the nudist colony?
"Stay out of my hair!"

If a man's wife is his better half, what's his mistress?
His better hole!

Why did the girl stand on the side of the road with her ass hanging out?
She was bumming a ride!

★

How can you tell if a maître d' likes you?
His staff springs into action!

★

What do you call oral sex in London?
English muffin'!

★

What does an alcoholic call his dog?
Liverspot!

★

Why did the guy chase his girlfriend up a tree?
So he could kiss her between the limbs!

★

What should a doctor do if his nurse is choking from a bone in her throat?
Pull it out!

★

Where did the honeymooning spiders stay?
In their newlyweb!

★

How do women get minks?
The same way that minks get minks!

★

What's 138?
Dinner for four!

What's the difference between a bartender and a proctologist?
A proctologist only has to look at one asshole at a time!

Why don't they have seat belts in the 1984 Cadillacs?
They replaced them with Velcro on the ceiling!

What did the psychiatrist say to the nymphomaniac?
"I can only offer you temporary relief!"

Why does a cannon roar?
You'd roar, too, if one of your balls was shot off!

How would you describe a pygmy prostitute?
"A little fucker about this high!"

Why is sex like potato salad?
Because if you share it, you have a picnic!

The biggest song hit of 1967 was . . .
(Check one)

_____ 1. *As I Kissed Her Ruby Lips, She Crossed Her Legs And Broke My Glasses*
_____ 2. *I Laid My Peach On The Beach And Got Sand In The Fuzz*
_____ 3. *Everything You Always Wanted To Know About Sex But Were Afraid To Eat*
_____ 4. *Sit On My Face And Let Me Guess Your Weight*
_____ 5. *Strangers In My Mouth*

What's the best indication that the bride should diet on the honeymoon?
(Check-out counter)

_____ 1. She walks down the aisle and sideswipes both families.
_____ 2. Everyone throws puffed rice.
_____ 3. You can't hear the band playing "Daddy's Little Girl" over the snickering.
_____ 4. She gets up to dance the polka and makes the band skip.
_____ 5. The groom throws her garter and lassos the best man.
_____ 6. The reception ends when the bride cuts the cheese.
_____ 7. The groom has to carry her over the threshold with a forklift.
_____ 8. She has her wedding portrait painted and the artist has to use a roller.

★

The gay choirboy . . .
(Chex wheat)

_____ 1. prayed for the second coming
_____ 2. polished the Bishop's knob
_____ 3. never got off on Sundays
_____ 4. tended to the heads of the congregation
_____ 5. choked on his first hymn

★

Why did the Polish girl stop wearing her training bra?
(Check her straps)

_____ 1. So her junior jugs could jiggle when she jogged.
_____ 2. To get to the other size.
_____ 3. Because air is free.
_____ 4. Her red-tipped hooters were too huge.
_____ 5. The wheels were irritating her armpits.

118

What was the most tasteless bumper sticker of 1973?
(Chink food)

_____ 1. "Movers Do It With Dollies"
_____ 2. "Mechanics Do It With Greasy Tools"
_____ 3. "Doctors Do It With Patience"
_____ 4. "Don't Let The Boss Crap All Over You! Open
         Your Mouth!"
_____ 5. "If It Wasn't For Imagination We'd All Be
         Happy"
_____ 6. "Masochists Do It For Kicks"
_____ 7. "DJ's Do It With Microphones"
_____ 8. "Save A Tree! Eat A Beaver!"

★

Linda Lovelace's most recent movie was . . .
(Check her out)

_____ 1. *Licking for Mr. Goodbar*
_____ 2. *Germs of Endearment*
_____ 3. *The Right Stiff*
_____ 4. *Rentyl*
_____ 5. *Airplane 69*
_____ 6. *Caddy Shack-up*

★

What's the most telltale sign that your wife is not into
love-making?
(Check her box often!)

_____ 1. A quickie before dinner is a short drink.
_____ 2. She thinks it's group sex if she helps.
_____ 3. You buy a tube of K-Y jelly and she puts it on the
         doorknob so you can't get in the bedroom.
_____ 4. You put a mirror over your bed and the next time
         the two of you are getting it on, you catch her
         popping zits.
_____ 5. She opens her legs and the oil burner goes on.

119

What are the three words a woman most likes to hear from her husband when he walks in the door from work?

(Check his coat)

_____ 1. "I love you!"
_____ 2. "Sorry I'm late!"
_____ 3. "Let's go out!"
_____ 4. "You've lost weight!"
_____ 5. "Here's my paycheck!"
_____ 6. "Roll a joint!"
_____ 7. "What gorgeous tits!"
_____ 8. "Suck my dick!"
_____ 9. "I'm getting hard!"
_____10. "Where's your clit?"
_____11. "Go fuck yourself!"

★

"I just flew in from Greece, and, boy! are my arms . . .

(Check what you think should go on the end!)

_____ 1. ". . . tired!"
_____ 2. ". . . hairy!!"
_____ 3. ". . . revolting!!!"
_____ 4. ". . . backwards!!!!"
_____ 5. ". . . sticky!!!!!"

★

The naive Italian son is getting married, and he asks his father what to do on his wedding night. The old man tells him to "put the hardest thing you've got in the place where she goes to the bathroom!" On the wedding night, the son proceeds to . . .

(Check the proper box!)

_____ 1. put his bocci ball in the sink
_____ 2. put his algebra book in the bathtub
_____ 3. stick his head in her skivvies
_____ 4. sit on the edge of the bed and wait for the swelling to go down
_____ 5. start screaming, "There's shit in this box!"

The most popular "obvious yes" answer of the sixties was . . .
(Chews one)

____ 1. "Are there any Jews in show business?"
____ 2. "Are San Francisco police mounted?"
____ 3. "Is Dr. Renee Richards dis-jointed?"
____ 4. "Does a Prague divorce lawyer ask for separate Czechs?"
____ 5. "Is life a four-letter word?"
____ 6. "Did Roy stuff Trigger?"
____ 7. "Does a gynecologist spread old wives' tails?"

★

Which of the following is potentially the most traumatic school experience?
(Check, please)

____ 1. Your junior high art teacher tells you that you could be another Van Gogh, and she hands you a knife.
____ 2. Your biology lab partner sides with the frog.
____ 3. The closest you come to a French kiss is a slow water fountain.
____ 4. Spending all of your recesses running from one end of the seesaw to the other.
____ 5. Your driver's ed teacher makes you chip in for gas.
____ 6. Your driver's ed teacher makes you blow him.
____ 7. Your driver's ed teacher makes you blow a gas station attendant.

When do you realize for sure that you're an unwanted child?

_____ 1. When you're descended from a long line that your mother once listened to

_____ 2. When your earliest memories are hitchhiking home from the hospital

_____ 3. When your mother lets you lick the beaters on her mixer and doesn't shut it off

_____ 4. When your only bath toys are a toaster and a radio

_____ 5. When your parents send you out on Halloween dressed as a speed bump

_____ 6. When your only Christmas present is a bat and it flies away

_____ 7. When your only Christmas present is a dart game with automatic return

_____ 8. When they bring you saltines after your tonsillectomy

_____ 9. When, after you're born, you get a ticket for leaving the scene of an accident

_____10. When you're baptized in boiling water

_____11. When your parents advertise for babysitters at the child-abuse clinic

★

A good secretary . . .
(Check when appropriate)

_____ 1. knows what's in the boss's drawers
_____ 2. never misses a period
_____ 3. is a hunt 'n pecker
_____ 4. doesn't file her nails (just throws them away)
_____ 5. isn't permanent until she's screwed on the desk

What's harder than getting a pregnant elephant into a Volkswagen?
(Check your oil)

_____ 1. Painting a fart blue
_____ 2. Putting it in soft
_____ 3. Saying "unique New York" three times fast
_____ 4. Word problems
_____ 5. Getting an elephant pregnant in a Volkswagen

★

Which of the following is the world's worst opening line?
(Check just one, but memorize the lot)

_____ 1. "You live around here often?"
_____ 2. "Nice day for weather!"
_____ 3. "Want to lock crotches and swap gravy?"
_____ 4. "Haven't I mentally undressed you somewhere before?"
_____ 5. "Are there any more at the home like you?"
_____ 6. "For a fat broad you don't sweat that much."
_____ 7. "Eric Weber has herpes!"
_____ 8. "Is it hot in here or is it you?"
_____ 9. "What's your signal? I'm a clitoris and last night I mooned in the House Of Pancakes."
_____10. "Can I try my bowling grip on you?"
_____11. "Go fuck yourself!"

III.

*What starts with "f," and ends with "k,"
and if you can't get one, you have to
use your hands??
Fork!!!*

What are the rules if you sleep with a Greek wrestler?
No holes barred!

★

What's the ecological statement found on Polish toilet paper?
"Save a tree! Use both sides!"

★

What do you get when you cross a gay with a pyromaniac?
A blow torch!

★

Why don't any Mexicans work in the space program?
Every time somebody says "launch" they sit down to eat!

★

What's the difference between a bowling ball and a girl?
You can only fit three fingers in a bowling ball!
How are they alike?
You see a marked improvement in your scoring when you get your own!

★

What happens if a guaranteed prophylactic breaks?
The guarantee runs out!

★

How do Italian girls learn to kiss so well?
From eating spaghetti with their hands tied behind their backs!

What's more perverted than walking around the city feeling all the telephone slots?
Having your jockey shorts personalized in Braille!

★

What happens if you lose at strip poker?
You wind up in the hole!

★

What's Black and sits on Trigger?
LeRoy Rogers!

★

Why do you always find a fly in cactus soup?
It's the only way to get the pricks out!

★

What did the priest say after the nun gave him a big, wet French kiss?
"This is one habit I'd definitely like to get into!"

★

Why is it hard to tell if two people are thinking of having a platonic relationship?
They don't do it!
When do platonic relationships work out for two people?
When it's play for one of them and tonic for the other!

★

How do dogs make love?
Everybody nose!

Why should you never buy your girlfriend a bicycle?
Because she'll peddle it all over town!

★

What's WASP foreplay?
Buying cigarettes!

★

Why did the gynecologist's wife leave him?
She found out he was seeing other women!

★

Why can't Frankenstein have any kids?
His nuts are in his neck!

★

What's worse than finding crackers in your bed?
Finding a crumb in your closet!

★

What's the ironic thing about pantyhose?
The bottom goes in the top!

★

What do you call it when you put your pecker on a girl's boobies?
Head for the hills!

★

What did the hooker say to the john who claimed he had thirteen inches?
"I find that hard to swallow!"

129

When do you know you have bad breath?
When you walk into your dentist's office and he gives *himself* a shot of Novocaine!

★

What would you call a male whorehouse?
A log cabin!

★

Why did they name the new feminine hygiene spray "S.S.Y.?"
Because it takes the "P.U." out of pussy!

★

What does a Black family say after they get home from a long trip?
"Home again, home again, jiggity jig!"

★

What did George M. Cohan say before he masturbated?
"The yanks are coming, the yanks are coming . . ."

★

What's the definition of a schmuck?
A schmuck is a guy who steps out of the shower to take a leak and won't undress in front of his dog!

★

What would you call Dolly Parton as a cowgirl?
Flopalong Cassidy!

★

Why did Donald Duck divorce Daisy?
Her quack was too big!

130

What does a Polish girl do when she's feeling sexy?
Winks at her vibrator!

What's the difference between a gigolo, a doctor, a rabbi, a girlfriend and a Quaalude?
A gigolo is a penis vendor, a doctor is a penis mender, a rabbi is a penis ender, a girlfriend is a penis tender and a Quaalude is a penis bender!

A girl joined a nudist colony where they only make love with their eyes. How did she get pregnant?
Obviously, one of the guys was cockeyed!

How many punk rockers does it take to change a light bulb?
Two. One to change the bulb, and one to kick the chair out from under him!

What's better than watching a girl wrestle?
Seeing her box!

★

How can you tell if a crab is sad?
It climbs up your leg and bawls!

★

What's the best thing about the new twin-engine economy jets?
If you lose an engine, you get to circle the place you're gonna hit!

What's the definition of a lady?
Someone who doesn't smoke, doesn't drink, and only curses when it slips out!

★

What's a faggot's favorite folk song?
Puff the Magic Dragon!

★

Penis ailin'?
Penicillin!

★

What's prune foo yung?
Chinese food to go!

★

What's the shortest distance between two points?
A tight blouse!

★

What's the definition of a great salesman?
A guy who can sell a suit with two pairs of pants to a flasher!

★

What's a "plutonic" love affair?
You only do it doggie-style!

★

Why is it a shame that the Pilgrims didn't shoot a bobcat?
Because then we'd all be eating pussy on Thanksgiving!

What should you call your father if he has pimples?
Pop!

★

What's a French chastity belt?
A catcher's mask!

★

Which new flavored douche is a sex stretcher?
Hairburger Helper!

★

Why did the Polack throw away his toilet brush?
He went back to using paper!

★

How can you tell if an artist is promiscuous?
She takes a licking every time she sells a painting!

★

Who's the world's greatest athlete?
A guy who finishes first and third in a masturbation contest!

★

What happened to the butcher who backed into his slicing machine?
He got a little behind in his work!

★

Why don't congressmen use bookmarks?
They prefer to bend over their pages!

What's the nicest thing a girl could give a man for his seventy-fifth birthday?
An erection!

★

How is Dolly Parton able to cope now that her husband has left her?
She still has her mammaries!

★

When a Greek gets married, what does he look forward to most?
His honey's moon!

★

What would you call a one-hour laxative mixed with fruit juice?
A clockwork orange!

★

What's a tease?
A girl who reclines before she declines!

★

If a bra is an "over the shoulder boulder holder," what's a jock strap?
An "under the butt nut hut!"

★

What's a sports mechanic?
A guy who fixes ball games!

How does a guy know he drank *way* too much the night before?
When he wakes up with a queer taste in his mouth!

What do you call hair on a hemorrhoid?
Pile carpet!

What's 68?
"Do me and I'll owe you one!"

What's the problem with a seven-day honeymoon?
It makes a whole week!

Why did the girl refuse to go to bed with the guy who was half French and half Greek?
Because she was afraid she wouldn't know which way to turn!

What's the first thing you do after a great date?
Brush your teeth with a comb!

If a guy has five willies, how does his underwear fit?
Like a glove!

What did the crew say when, after eleven weeks at sea, Columbus yelled "Eureka!"
"You don't smell so hot yourself!"

What's the worst thing about dating a grandmother?
You have to look in every nook and cranny to find the cranny with the nooky!

What does an Italian artist draw?
Flies!

What's a gay exhibitionist's favorite folk song?
Blowin' in the Window!

Why shouldn't you wear soundproof shorts?
You'll never hear the end of it!

What would you call a housing development for the Moral Majority?
God's Belly Acres!

Why did the swallow fly upside-down?
For a lark!

What's the fastest speed at which you can make love?
68! Because at 69 you have to turn around and go the other way!

What do you have when your girlfriend calls you up and gets you excited?
A telebone!

What did the faggot do at the ball game?
Had a couple of Franks!

Why do men love to jerk off?
It's the only time they talk to themselves and get a straight
answer!

When did the madam realize that the guy with no arms and
legs on the front porch of the brothel wasn't fooling around?
When she figured out how he rang the doorbell!

What's the square root of 69?
Eight something!

Why can't crows make love quietly?
Caws!

Why doesn't it matter if one of a girl's nipples is off-center?
It's beside the point!

How can you tell Jesus was Jewish?
He went into his father's business!

What did the Polack do when his girl told him she had her
menstrual cycle?
Went over on his moped!

137

Why was the man-eating tiger licking his asshole?
He had just eaten a Polack and was trying to get the taste out of his mouth!

What would you call a singles bar for senior citizens?
Shufflebroads!

Why do they say that a man is not complete until he's married?
Because then he's finished!

Why did the Greek take his wife on his business trip?
Because he couldn't leave her behind alone!

Where do cousins come from?
Antholes!

What do you give an elephant with diarrhea?
Lots of room!

When do you know your sex life is really hurting?
When reaching for change lifts your spirits!

What did Cinderella sing to her impotent lover?
"Someday my prince will come!"

What's green and has a trunk?
A seasick tourist!

★

What would they call a sitcom based on *Deep Throat*?
Oral in the Family!

★

Why wasn't the teenage boy embarrassed when his father caught him jerking off?
Because the old man came into his room looking for tissues!

★

What did the girl say to her date when he couldn't get an erection?
"You're better off!"

★

Why don't they put Howard Cosell on a postage stamp?
They're afraid everyone will spit on the wrong side!

★

How do you know the Greek on the subway?
He's the one backing into the turnstile!

★

Why did the divorcee want to get a job at the sex change clinic?
So she could meet a lot of new men!

★

Is it okay for a high school boy to masturbate?
Yes, as long as it's not against his principal!

139

What's the best place in town to take a leak?
A radiator shop!

What's better than honor?
In her!

How could you tell that the swan was horny?
Because he shot off across the lake!

What did the Polack say before he committed hara-kiri?
"If I don't get this right, I'm gonna kill myself!"

What's the difference between a counterfeit dollar bill and a skinny girl?
A counterfeit dollar bill is a phony buck!

What's the worst thing about dating a girl who has asthma?
When you're fucking her it sounds like she's hissing you!

★

What did the little girl do when her mother wouldn't let her lick the bowl?
Flushed it!

★

Why did the salesman like his new female boss?
She gave him a raise!

140

What did the dentist say to the lady after she told him she'd rather have a baby than have a tooth pulled?
"Make up your mind, I have to adjust the chair!"

★

How do you know when you're in a *very* small town?
When the local hooker has herpe!

★

How does a sorority girl know if her roommate enjoyed her date?
If she throws her panties and they stick to the ceiling!

★

What did the midget do in the gay bar?
Kissed everybody in the joint!

★

Is sex better than pot?
It depends on the pusher!

★

If a woman is a nymphomaniac, what is her husband?
Tired!

★

What happens if you don't pay your exorcist?
You get repossessed!

★

What does a girl call head in the afternoon?
Lunch!

Where can you find a couple of gay snowmen?
On an icicle built for two!

Why is sex so popular?
Because it's centrally located!

Why did the nymphomaniac only make love doggie-style?
It was the only position her doggie knew!

What weighs two thousand pounds and swims in San Francisco Bay?
Moby Dyke!

Is sex a misdemeanor?
Sure! De more you miss, de meaner you get!

What's worse, being Black or gay?
Gay. You don't have to tell your mother that you're Black!

What did the Polish girl say to the X-rated comic?
"I don't care if your jokes are clever, as long as they're dirty!"

What did the booger say to Kermit?
"It's not easy being green!"

What's an industrial-strength antacid capsule?
Janitor in a Tum!

When does a guy know it's been a long time since he's had any sexual action?
When he can't remember which armpit it's under!

What do you call graffiti in the ladies's room?
Squatters' writes!

What did Cinderella say to Pinnochio when she sat on his face?
"Tell a lie . . . tell the truth . . . tell a lie . . . tell the truth . . ."

How can you tell if a parrot is gay?
If he likes a cockatoo!

What are Brownie points?
New boobs on a Girl Scout!

If your arm gets broken in two places, what should you do?
Stay out of those two places!

How can you tell if a woman is experienced?
She knows when she shouldn't cough!

Who's the bravest man in the world?
A peanut vendor! He whistles while his nuts are roasting!

What would you call a beginner pimp?
A rookie nookie bookie!

Why is Billie Jean King so good at tennis?
Because she can swing both ways!

Why did the nymphomaniac commit a crime?
So she could be tried by a jury!

How did the college student find out his roommate was gay?
It came as quite a blow to him!

What's the definition of "macho?"
Jogging home from your vasectomy!

What did the faggot say when he was brushing his teeth and
his gums started to bleed?
"Safe for another month!"

Why did the sea gull fly over Hollywood and Vine?
He wanted to try and spot a movie star!

How do you know the bachelors at the nudist colony?
They're up for grabs!

Why is sex better than golf?
You don't have to ask the caddy which club to use!

What would you call a hooker with no arms and legs?
A night crawler!

Why are Jewish children so obnoxious?
Heredity!

What did the Polish general do when he heard that
Napoleon wore red into battle so his troops wouldn't panic
in the event he was wounded?
Ordered a brown uniform!

What would you call a gay arsonist?
A flaming faggot!

If you don't score on your first date with a girl, what should
you do?
Take another whack at it!

What's the scariest thing for a nudist?
Frying bacon!

145

Why did the girl quit her job as artist for the zipper company?
She was sick and tired of drawing flies!

★

How did the telephone operator's husband get pregnant?
She reversed the charges!

★

Why was the cheerleader black and blue from gonorrhea?
She gave it to one of the football players!

★

When does a circus tent leak?
When the man on the flying trap-pees!

★

What gets wetter as it dries?
Toilet paper!

★

What do you get when you cross a telephone operator with an old battery?
A call girl who doesn't charge!

★

What did the hotel operator say to Prince Charles when she called to wake him and his new bride?
"Up Chuck and Di!"

★

Who visits Michael Jackson on Christmas Eve?
Crisco Kringle!

What's the definition of a henpecked husband?
A guy who doesn't know how to tell his pregnant wife that
he's sterile!

★

What's a basketball team with no sex?
The New York Eunuchs!

★

What do you give an eighty-five-year-old lady for her
birthday?
Mikey! He'll eat anything!

★

Why did the first-grade girl cry when she saw her first report
card?
She got an "F" in sex and she didn't even know she was
taking it!

★

Why did the Italian girl's boyfriend carry her books for her?
She couldn't cover the bets herself!

★

Why should you think twice before you marry a girl with
hair down to her waist and boobs that stick out?
Because in ten years her boobs will be down to her waist
and her hair will stick out!

★

Why did God give Jews big noses?
Because He knew that they would be the only ones that
could afford cocaine!

147

What's the difference between a golf course and intercourse?
Intercourse has the hole in the middle of the rough!

Why didn't the fly stay on the toilet seat?
He got pissed off!

Why can't you shake hands with the world's greatest lover?
He always has a boob in it!

Why does a fireman wear a red jock strap?
To hold up his hose!

What did the clerk ask the groom as he was signing the register for the bridal suite?
"How long do you plan to stay in it?"

What would you call an Irish anteater?
An uncle!

Why did the narcissistic contortionist stop struggling?
Because he finally came into his own!

What's a gay farm boy's favorite pastime?
Playing stoop tag in the asparagus patch!

148

What would you call the tallest comedian in the shower room?
Top banana!

★

Why did they arrest the naked mummy?
No gauze at all!

★

What do you call a meal of chicken served with lima beans and corn?
Cock succotash!

★

If the answer is "bitter end," what is the question?
What did you do when the pretty girl mooned you?

★

What are the two stages of being a husband?
When you want to be faithful but are not, and when you want to be unfaithful but cannot!

★

What would you call a hooker with a runny nose?
Full!

★

What's the worst problem a man can have with sex and booze?
Every time he has sex, the girl boos!

★

If the plural of kitty is kitties, what's the plural of pussy?
Harem!

How can you tell the promiscuous girl in biology class?
While everyone else is dissecting frogs, she's opening flies!

What's a rubber egg beater?
A condom!

Why can't a man win with his wife?
Because if he comes home early, she accuses him of being horny. If he comes home late, she suspects that he's been out getting it. And if he comes home on time, she figures he got it already!

What's the wildest thing you can do in a movie theatre?
Get a blowjob in the no-smoking section!

Why did the pervert take the Girl Scout home?
So she could get her cookies!

★

What's the best way to watch a romantic movie?
Hand in gland, gland in hand!

★

What's a shoe fetishist?
A guy that looks down when you say, "What a pair!"

★

What did the girl say to the guy at the bar when he told her he wanted to get in her pants?
"Go ahead! There's one ass in there already!"

Why couldn't the Frenchman's wife get pregnant?
He kept muffing it!

★

Is it true that a girl can attract a man with her mind?
Yes. But she can attract more men with what she doesn't
mind!

★

How do you keep a fag from getting pregnant?
Burp him!

★

How do you find out if your date is ticklish?
Give her a couple of test tickles!

★

Why do women over fifty make great dates?
They don't yell, they don't tell, they don't swell, and
they're grateful as hell!

★

What's brown and crispy on the outside, and white and
creamy on the inside?
A cockroach!

★

Why is marriage like a warm toilet seat?
It's comfortable, but you never know who was there before
you!

★

Why did the Polack marry the dog?
He had to!

What's the distance between a girl's legs?
A fur piece!

What should a girl read if she's worried that her boyfriend might be getting into golden showers?
Looking Out for #1!

What would a married woman's life be like without her husband?
The same, with one small exception!

What did the gay commuter's roommate holler as he jerked off into a rubber early one morning?
"I'm packing your lunch!"

Why can't gigolos get steady employment?
They only work in spurts!

What do you get when you cross a rooster with a telephone pole?
A cock that wants to reach out and touch someone every morning at daybreak!

What did the husband say to his wife after she told him that she just had quadruplets?
"That's enough out of you!"
What did she name them?
Adolph, Rudolph, Get Off and Stay Off!

What do you call a girl that loses the string to her tampon?
A cotton picker!

What did the girl say as she rode her bike over a cobblestone street?
"I'll never come this way again!"

What's the quietest place in the world?
The complaint department at the parachute-packing plant!

What does a gay whale do to get his jollies?
Bites the ends off submarines and sucks out all the seamen!

Why did the magician saw his wife in half?
He couldn't stand her whole!

What does a weight lifter do in the shower?
Clean and jerk!

What's the difference between poverty and a Jewish bride?
You can get used to poverty!

How do you order a cherry Dr Pepper?
"One virgin surgeon!"

What's black and white and red all over?
A pinstripe Kotex!

What do they do in a Polish restaurant when you order the chef's salad?
Bring you the one he was eating!

How can you tell if a dog has herpes?
Won't heal!

Why is a gay guy like a letter?
They both come in the mail!

How can you tell if a woman is having an orgasm?
Who cares?

What's a quarter of an inch long and likes to lick young boys' sweaty testicles?
Uncle Ben's Perverted Rice!

★

What's a nice name for a pimp?
A fornicaterer!

★

Why do girls rub their eyes when they wake up in the morning?
Because they don't have testicles!

What did the doctor say when he realized he was trying to write a prescription with his thermometer?
"Jesus Christ! Some asshole has my pen!"

Why was the bisexual prizefighter undefeated?
He could lick anybody!

Why are Visine eye drops like Tampax?
They both get the red out!

Why was the girl patting her date on the forehead with a feather?
Because he had told her he was going to fuck her to death, and, relatively speaking, she was beating his brains out!

What did Adam do after he found Eve's beneath the leaves?
Started a fad that makes us all glad!

How can you tell if a Boy Scout is mean?
He walks little old ladies *halfway* across the street!

Why is it hard to say "oragenitalism?"
Because it's a mouthful!

What do you call a Black guy who sells Preparation H?
An ass-cream coon!

Why is a virgin like a balloon?
One prick and it's all over!

★

What was God's intention for pubic hair?
Organic dental floss!

★

What's a liberated woman?
A woman who had sex before marriage and a job afterwards!

★

Why do women get married?
So they can settle down and take root!

★

How do you know when two dogs are in love?
They're hung up on each other!

★

Why are gays so confusing?
Because they're up when they're down!

★

What's a Jewish pervert?
A guy that wants to get into his *mother's* business!

★

Why do girl preppies have alligators on their underwear?
It's closer to the swamp!

★

Why is England's flag like the Queen's skirt?
They both go up for the King!

Why is 77 better than 69?
You get eight more!

What's a hobosexual?
A fucking bum!

Who has the world's best memory?
A person that can remember going to a party with his father
and coming home with his mother!

Where do most men stand when it comes to masturbation?
The shower!

How would Dirty Johnny use the word "contagious" in a
sentence?
"As my sister gets older, her contagious!"

What's the difference between a gynecologist and a proctologist?
Only their point of view!

Why don't they serve calves' brains at United Negro
College Fund banquets?
Because the mind is a terrible thing to baste!

★

What's better than playing the piano by ear?
Fiddling with your pecker!

If an "eight" gives great head, and a "ten" swallows, what's a "twelve?"
A girl who gargles!

★

What charity do Michael Jackson and Richard Pryor support?
The Ignited Negro College Fund!

★

How can you tell if a part-time gas jockey enjoyed his high school prom?
There's lipstick on his dipstick!

★

What's the sex education primer?
Fun Dickin' Jane!

★

What's the difference between a rooster and a horny girl?
A rooster goes "cock-a-doodle-doo," and a horny girl goes "any cock'll do!"

★

Why is pubic hair curly?
So it won't poke you in the eye!

★

What's sodomy?
Something any ass can do!

★

What did Roy Rogers get when he made love to Trigger?
Horseshoe crabs!

How do you scare a Black guy?
Give the jigaboo!

Why did the girl take her vibrator to the beach?
So she could shake and bake!

What do you call it when an acupuncturist works on testicles?
Stickball!

Why do girls fart after they pee?
They can't shake it so they blow it dry!

Why shouldn't couples buy water beds?
They'll drift apart!

What did the college girl's mother say when her daughter told her she was in bed with hepatitis?
"Don't let him flip you over!"

What would you call a Black guy that stutters?
A cocoon!

Who's the most popular guy at the nudist masquerade party?
The guy that comes dressed as a gasoline pump!

159

What does it prove if you go down on a girl while she
tickles you with a feather?
That you can have your kink and eat it, too!

★

What did James Watt get for Christmas?
Laces for his pacifier!

★

Why did the well-hung contortionist have trouble talking to
people?
Because he was always putting his foot in his mouth!

★

How does a gay spell relief?
N-O-A-I-D-S!

★

What would you call an ugly girl who gives head?
A lap dog!

★

How can you tell if a guy is a masochist?
He beats his meat with a hammer!

★

How can you tell if Dolly Parton forgot to wear her bra?
There are no wrinkles in her face!

★

What's the difference between a pig and a musician?
A pig won't stay up all night trying to fuck a musician!

When do you know your dandruff is out of control?
When your crabs have to wear snowshoes!

How can you tell if a mounted cop is absent-minded?
He jumps on his whistle and blows his horse!

Why did the college boy kick his gay roommate out of the house?
He said he was a pain in the ass!

What did the psychiatrist say to the patient who claimed to have an irresistible urge to stuff his nostrils full of tobacco?
"Want a light?"

Why do girls use genital spray?
For around-the-cock protection!

What did Adam say when he woke up and was missing a rib?
"Something smells fishy around here!"

What do you call people that watch Dick Van Dyke reruns over and over?
Mary Tyler Morons!

How can you tell if two gay men are clumsy?
They bump heads!

Why didn't the invisible man and the invisible woman have any children?
They went to Planned Transparenthood!

Why did the cat watch the tennis match so closely?
His old man was in the racket!

What does the Lone Ranger do in the men's room after a big meal?
Take a dump, take a dump, take a dump dump dump!

Why does an Italian girl never wear panties?
To keep the flies off her moustache!

What's the difference between herpes and AIDS?
Herpes is a love story; AIDS is a fairy tale!

What should a man do once he's learned to read women like a book?
Use his fingers to mark his place!

Why does Liz Taylor keep her Christmas stocking on the mantle year-round?
To hold the firewood!

How do you know if you were built upside-down?
Your nose runs and your feet smell!

162

Why are American Express Card holders always late?
Because they never leave home without it!

Why did the girl ask her date to put two fingers in her?
She wanted to whistle!

What would you call a computerized toilet bowl?
A turd processor!

What's a platonic relationship?
A relationship between a guy who wants to have sex and a girl who doesn't!

What did the girl say after her date with the invisible man?
"I never knew what I was up against!"

What's the best thing about dating a movie usher?
He can find your seat in the dark!

When should you throw away a girl's phone number?
If she gives you head and leaves a ring!

Why is a penis like a payday?
It can't come too often!

What's red and white and falls down the chimney?
Santa Klutz!

What's the best thing about a convention of comediennes?
All the funny cracks!

★

If marriage is a wonderful institution, why do so many couples get divorced?
They realize they don't like living in an institution!

★

What do you call oral sex in a national park?
Old faceful!

★

What's honeymoon salad?
Lettuce alone!

★

What happened to the robot that crossed the mob?
They put out a service contract on it!

★

What's the difference between a sewing machine and a girl in a tight sweater?
The sewing machine only has one bobbin!

★

Why did the cowboy fuck the buffalo?
He had never heard a discouraging word!

★

What did the two crickets do on their honeymoon?
Hopped to it!

Why did the cheerleader strip?
So she could go "rah rah" raw!

What monster do you find in the laundry room?
The wash-and-wearwolf!

What would you call it when a faggot shoves a live gerbil up his ass?
An enemal!

What did the masochistic girl say to her date?
"Slap, or I'll stop you!"

Why in the traditional wedding picture is the groom in a chair and the bride standing?
Because he's too tired to get up, and she's too sore to sit down!

★

What do you call oral sex on the West Coast?
L.A.-tio!

★

What do you get if you eat uranium?
You get atomic ache!

★

What should you do if your girlfriend tells you that picking your nose is disgusting?
Do it yourself!

What's black and white and climbs the walls?
A virgin penguin!

Why wasn't the Polack worried when his brakes gave out?
He was coming to a stop sign!

What's the difference between a white ladies' man and a
Black ladies' man?
A white ladies' man walks right up and puts it in; a Black
ladies' man puts it in and then walks right up!

What's the last thing you should try to do when you take a
girl parking?
Borrow money from her for the meter!

What did the Indian say when he saw the mushroom cloud
from the A-bomb test?
"Wishum *I* had said that!"

What does an Eskimo lesbian eat?
Cold cuts!

Why isn't it smart to have a thoroughbred gelded until his
racing days are over?
Because when the announcer screams "They're off!" they
drop dead from embarrassment!

What does "gelded" mean?
It's Latin for "They're off!"

166

What makes a horse a thoroughbred?
He understands Latin!

How can you tell if someone is full of shit?
They pretend the last few jokes made any sense!

Why is making love to your girlfriend like cleaning your room?
Because no matter how good a job you do, you're eventually going to have to do it again!

What should a man do before he takes a wife?
Find out whose wife it is he's taking!

Why did the Polish girl return the mirror that was installed over her bed?
There was a crack in it!

What's a prophylactic?
A planned parent hood!

★

Where can you go to see a man eating pussy?
The lion's cage at the zoo!

★

What's the definition of trust?
Two cannibals having oral sex!

What's the difference between a cow and a dyke?
Ten pounds and a flannel shirt. The cow may occasionally smile.

What's worse than picking up the soap in the Army shower?
Playing leapfrog in the Greek Navy!

Which toes do girls like to be scratched between?
The two big ones!

What would you call a castle full of semen?
Kingdom come!

What could you say about a guy who broke up with an Indian maiden for a Harlem hooker?
That he was out of the red and into the black!

How can you tell if a New York City bum has a good rap?
The pigeons are throwing bread crumbs to *him*!

Why did the male stripper get fired?
He didn't have the hang of it!

Why does Ronald Reagan have to be careful shaving?
So he doesn't accidentally circumcise his neck!

How do you know when you're really boring?
Girls sit on your face just to shut you up!

★

What's the one drawback to oral sex?
The view!

★

What's green and skates backwards?
Peggy Phlegm!

★

How can you tell if a bride is sleepy?
She can't stay awake for a second!

★

What's a ratchet?
A little bigger than a moushet!

★

Where does a Polish girl keep her diaphragm?
Tacked over the headboard!

★

How many lesbians does it take to screw in a light bulb?
Four. One to screw it in, and three to discuss how it's so
much more gratifying than with a man!

★

Why is it dumb for a man to burn the candle at both ends?
It makes it too hard to keep his wife in the dark!

★

What would you call a Canadian policeman who moonlights
as a gigolo?
Mountie Python!

What happened when the farmer crossed the rooster with the Spanish fly?
The hens got a big bang out of it!

How can you tell if a girl bathes in vinegar?
She's the one with the sour puss!

How many fleas does it take to screw in a light bulb?
Two! But first, you have to get them into the light bulb!

What does a prostitute call her earnings?
John dough!

Who was a heavyweight champion with a flatulence problem?
Gaseous Clay!

Why don't Polish guys smoke pot?
It's too painful to light their joints!

How can you tell if a masochist is gay?
He's a sucker for punishment!

Why did the girl cross crickets and crabs?
She wanted to have a music box!

170

What should you do if a waitress sits on your hand?
Try to get her off!

What's the most ironic thing that ever happened on Fire Island?
A fellow getting a bone caught in his throat while he was eating blowfish!

What would you call a Jewish country singer?
Nashville Katz!

How does a Polish couple make love doggie-style?
He sniffs her ass and she growls!

What did the Chinese girl say when she slid down the banister?
"Holee smokee!"

How do you circumcise a whale?
Send down fore skin divers!

What does the sign inside a whorehouse say?
"No smoking! Use a lubricant!"

What does Dr. Joyce Brothers use for birth control?
Her face!

Why is credit like sex?
Because the people who need it the worst can't get it!

How can you tell if a gopher is bi-sexual?
He digs everybody's hole!

How can you tell if your Avon Lady is Polish?
She doesn't ring your bell; she tinkles on your lawn!

What did the madam say to the hookers?
"Let's get cracking!"

Why do skinny girls tease their hair?
To keep their pants up!

What do you do if you want to see flying saucers?
Go into an all-night diner and goose the waitresses!

Why was the gynecologist unemployed?
No openings!

How can you tell if a faggot is tough?
His poodle's name is Spike!

★

How did the Polack almost kill himself shooting craps?
The bullet richocheted off the porcelain!

172

Why doesn't Nancy Reagan ever tell Ronnie when she's having an orgasm?
Because he's never there!

★

Which of the following is going to be Kenny Rogers's last hit in his fourth *Best of* concoction?
(Please check)

_____ 1. *She Sits Among The Cabbages And Peas*
_____ 2. *You Can Keep The Girls Out Of The Sticks, But You Can't Keep The Sticks Out Of The Girls*
_____ 3. *Just Because I've Been Here Before Doesn't Mean I'm Not Lost Again*
_____ 4. *Come In Out Of The Wheatfield, Grandma, You're Goin' Against the Grain*
_____ 5. *You Picked A Fine Time To Leave Me, You Pig*

★

What would you call an insane Chinaman?
(Check one from column A. No substitutions!)

_____ 1. Wing Nut
_____ 2. Clay Z.
_____ 3. Chop Screwie
_____ 4. Egg Fool Yung
_____ 5. Folly Chan
_____ 6. Tonto

★

Which is the best all-time expression for women's breasts?
(Point)

_____ 1. boobs
_____ 2. red-tipped hooters
_____ 3. jugs
_____ 4. tits
_____ 5. knockers
_____ 6. gazumbas

What's better than meeting your girl in the park?
(Check your coat)

_____ 1. Parking your meat in a girl
_____ 2. Dressing up like a chicken
_____ 3. Getting a blowjob from a girl
_____ 4. Getting a blowjob from a chicken
_____ 5. Go fuck yourself!

★

Who was the first Jewish astronaut?
(Checky Greene)

_____ 1. Nose Cohen
_____ 2. Hymie to the Moon
_____ 3. Jon Glenn
_____ 4. Alice Kramden
_____ 5. José Jimeniwitcz

★

What was the most tasteless bumper sticker of 1981?
(Pick it and it will never heal)

_____ 1. "Electronic Surveillance Experts Do It With Bugs"
_____ 2. "(516) 922-WINE Fans Do It With Their Fingers"
_____ 3. "Fishermen Do It With Flies"
_____ 4. "Sardine Packers Do It In The Can"
_____ 5. "Reach Out And Fuck Someone Over"
_____ 6. "Did John Smith Pocahontas?"
_____ 7. "Fight The Population Explosion! Use Your Head!"
_____ 8. "Wine Tasters Spit It Out!"

What sign are you most likely to see at Planned Parenthood?
(Check ers)

_____ 1. "Thanks For Not Coming!"
_____ 2. "Use Rear Entrance!"
_____ 3. "Stop Your Kidding!"
_____ 4. "Be Careful Pulling Out!"
_____ 5. "Use Your Head!"

★

When do you know you're *really* horny?
(Check, check, check)

_____ 1. You have a cigarette after you stuff the Thanksgiving turkey.
_____ 2. Your own tongue starts to feel good in your mouth.
_____ 3. You pull off on the side of the road.
_____ 4. You rush to Sears when you hear that women's pants are half off.
_____ 5. Your psychiatrist asks you if you can remember the first time you masturbated and you can't remember the first time you'd masturbated *that day*!

★

When do you know that you're *really* flat-chested?
(Check when appropriate)

_____ 1. When your baby has to nurse with a straw
_____ 2. When you put your bra on backwards and it fits
_____ 3. When they elect you poster girl for the International House Of Pancakes
_____ 4. When your training bra gets a dishonorable discharge
_____ 5. When the highlight of your figure is your Adam's apple
_____ 6. When men tell you that they've seen more meat on a busboy's vest

175

_____ 7. When you have to go to a party topless just to get ignored

_____ 8. When your movie dates look at you and then buy Milk Duds

★

Example:
So I said to my wife with no legs,
" DOLLY ..."

1. So I said to my wife early one morning,
"_____ ..."

2. So I said to my wife after her car accident,
"_____ ..."

3. So I said to my wife when she fell playing tennis,
"_____ ..."

4. So I said to my wife as I took out my pecker,
"_____ ..."

5. So I said to my wife with the cocaine,
"_____ ..."

6. So I said to my wife with the space between her teeth, "_____ ..."

7. So I said to my wife who was real short,
"_____ ..."

8. So I said to my wife, the dwarf,
"_____ ..."

9. So I said to my wife as she let an incredible fart,
"_____ ..."

10. So I said to my wife who just got back from Paris,
"_____ ..."

11. So I said to my wife who was a tad bit overweight,
"_____ ..."

Choose from these answers:

a. "Edith ..." . . .   g. "Francine ..." . . .
b. "Gail ..." . . .   h. "Bridgette ..." . . .
c. "Sue ..." . . .   i. "Consuello ..." . . .
d. "Minnie ..." . . .   j. "Cher ..." . . .
e. "Wanda ..." . . .   k. "Courtney ..." . . .
f. "Dawn ..." . . .   l. "Penelope ..." . . .
m. "You fat God damn pig, stop eating ..." . . .

176

You can pick your nose, and you can pick your friends, but you can't . . .
(Check the proper passage)

_____ 1. pick your friend's nose
_____ 2. eat your friends
_____ 3. wipe your friends on the couch
_____ 4. wipe the fingerprints off
_____ 5. wait until the next multiple-guess joke
_____ 6. go fuck yourself

★

The most popular expression for male masturbation is . . .
(Checking off)

_____ 1. choking the chicken
_____ 2. running off a batch
_____ 3. jerkin' your gherkin
_____ 4. squeezin' the weasel
_____ 5. waxin' the carrot
_____ 6. buffin' the bishop
_____ 7. pulling your pud
_____ 8. burpin' the worm

★

Match the person's job with a typical comment from his bedroom. (See next page)

1. Delivery man . . . . _____
2. Politician . . . . _____
3. Interior decorator . . . . _____
4. Fireman . . . . _____
5. Dentist . . . . _____
6. Comedian . . . . _____
7. Usher . . . . _____
8. Salvation Army officer . . . . _____

a. "Stub, please!"
b. "You better let out some more hose! You're not close enough to the fire!"
c. "Anything would be appreciated!"
d. "I don't understand! It worked last night!"
e. "Ping-Pong balls? I thought you said 'King Kong's balls!'"
f. "Once I'm in . . ."
g. "Open wide for me . . ."
h. "Front or rear?"
i. "Check-um for bees!"
j. "How do you like it, now that it's up?"

★

The most popular "obvious yes" answer of the seventies was . . .
(Check only the ones that are)

_____ 1. "Is there fish on a Frenchman's breath?"
_____ 2. "Does a Fire Island boys' school have a headmaster?"
_____ 3. "Is a rim-job tongue in cheek?"
_____ 4. "Do lesbians kiss on the lips?"
_____ 5. "Is poon tangy?"
_____ 6. "Do backwards children need reversible roller skates?"

★

Which of the following is the favorite expression for a fart?
(Choose his food well)

_____ 1. Blooter
_____ 2. Tug a rug
_____ 3. Crack a rat
_____ 4. Rip the crackers
_____ 5. Toss a boom into the wind
_____ 6. Trouser cough
_____ 7. Toot
_____ 8. Blow a hole in your parachute
_____ 9. Cut the cheese

NO ARMS, NO LEGS!

What would you call a guy with no arms and no legs in the fireplace?
Bernie!
A little later?
Ashley!

What would you call a guy with no arms and no legs in a cartoon?
Drew!

What would you call a guy with no arms and no legs in a spice rack?
Herb! (Basil?)

What would you call a guy with no arms and no legs on a barbecue?
Frank!
His girlfriend?
Pattie!

What would you call a guy with no arms and no legs in a pile of leaves?
Russell!

★

What would you call a guy with no arms and no legs who you can walk under?
Arch!

What would you call a guy with no arms and no legs in a meat grinder?
Chuck!

★

What would you call a guy with no arms and no legs on top of soil?
Pete!

★

What would you call a guy with no arms and no legs in an avalanche?
Doug!

★

What would you call a girl with no arms and no legs on the beach?
Sandy!
If she was in the water?
Sandy Dunkin'!

★

Newly Elected to the Comedy Hall of Fame

Why is a lady like an airplane?
They both have cockpits!

★

What does "virgin wool" mean?
The sheep are just a little bit faster than the shepherds!

★

What do you get when you cross an Eskimo with a Puerto Rican homosexual?
A snow blower that won't work!

What did the elephant say to the naked man?
"How do you eat with that thing?"

How does a French woman hold her liquor?
By the ears!

Why is there a head on a penis?
To keep your hand from sliding off!

Who sweeps the ocean floor?
Jacques Custodian!

What do you get when you cross a faggot with a milkman?
A dairy queen!

Why is sex like a bank account?
Because you lose interest after withdrawal!

Why did the sailor reenlist?
He couldn't bear to leave his buddies behind!

What would you call a Puerto Rican in a Park Avenue penthouse?
A burglar!

What do you have if you have a mothball in your left hand
and a mothball in your right hand?
A huge moth, right where you want him!

Why does California have earthquakes and New York have
Blacks?
California had first choice!

What's the best thing to come out of a hard penis?
The wrinkles!

What do you get when you cross a Polack with a Cuban?
Ricky Retardo!

If storks bring babies, what kind of birds *don't* bring babies?
Swallows!

How did Helen Keller go bonkers?
Trying to read a stucco wall!

What's better than roses on your piano?
Tulips on your organ!

What's the difference between a Jewish American Princess
and a barracuda?
Nail polish!

182

What would you call a Vietnamese family with a dog?
Vegetarians!

What's four miles long and has an asshole every two feet?
The St. Patrick's Day Parade!

How did the garbage man get rich?
Catering Italian weddings!

When do you eat beans on Saturday night?
When you want to take a bubble bath Sunday morning!

WIN A FREE ALBUM!

Send your best jokes, riddles and rhymes!
Any jokes I can use on "516-922-WINE" will win one of
my LP's or cassettes (please specify)!
For response, send self-addressed, stamped envelope.
For more information and a free three-color "Use Your
Finger" sticker, also send a self-addressed, stamped enve-
lope.
Send it all to:

Jackie "922-WINE" Martling
Box 62
East Norwich, NY 11732

"Use Your Finger! 516-922-WINE!" has been different
every day for over five years, and many, many jokes have
already been on. But don't be discouraged! Give it your best
shot!
If I can't use your joke(s), I'll send you a discount coupon
good towards the purchase of any of my albums!

About the Author

Jackie "922-WINE" Martling has been a professional entertainer since the age of fourteen. He started playing in a pre-Beatles rock-and-roll band, played all through his schooling at Michigan State University (mechanical engineering, '71), continued in a Long Island-based comedy/original music trio, and made the switch to stand-up in 1979.

Jackie has released four party albums on his own *Off Hour Rockers Records*, all recorded live at his performances. *Just Another Dirty Joke Book*, his first in a series for *Pinnacle*, is selling like pancakes.

Jackie also owns and operates "Use Your Finger! 922-WINE," the world's only X-rated joke line (516-922-9463). The laugh line, which operates around the clock, is a minute of sassy, saucy jokes, rhymes and riddles that Jackie and his production partner Nancy Sirianni change faithfully seven days a week.

Jackie insists that his family is middle class on a good day, lives on the beautiful North Shore of Long Island, New York, and sees more laughs in his future.

Over 5,000,000 copies in print!

Larry Wilde

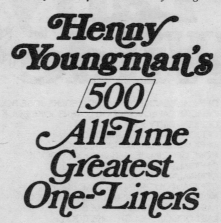